The First Epistle of John

The First Epistle of John

by

Albert Leckie

PRECIOUS SEED PUBLICATIONS

© Precious Seed Publications 2019
34 Metcalfe Avenue, Killamarsh, Sheffield, S21 1HW, UK

ISBN: 978-1-871642-92-6

Printed in the UK

Preface

A few words regarding the fact that this book is being published thirty years after Albert Leckie was called home to be with the Lord might help the reader to appreciate its contents and format.

For nearly thirty years Mr. Leckie conducted the Trimsaran Bible Readings in south west Wales. These were held in August each year and proved to be helpful to many believers in their understanding of a wide range of truth. In the mid-1970s the Readings were devoted to the study of John's Epistles. These have been transcribed and edited into a form suitable for publication and this book is the result.

Mr. Leckie felt that 1 John was a misunderstood book and his clear expositional and practical teaching will afford real help to the reader. This book contains many glorious themes of truth in respect of the person and work of our Lord Jesus Christ and the fellowship with divine persons that is enjoyed by the children of God. The book will remind an older generation of the rich ministry enjoyed from our brother and establish younger believers in the faith once for all delivered to us. Because of the way the book has been prepared, it has not been possible to include any bibliography or references. It is unlikely that everything in this book is original but the reader will discover delightful lines of truth not commonly expressed elsewhere.

Strenuous efforts have been made to discover the whereabouts of our brother's notes, particularly those bound in Oxford Loose Leaf Bible covers, but they have not been successful. A further plea is made that if their whereabouts are known they be made available to assist in future publications.

The publishers are grateful to John Stock for making available recordings of the Bible Readings, to Jemima Townsend and Matthew Cordiner for valued assistance in transcribing the recordings.

This is the third book in this series, following on from *Romans 1-8* and *The Tabernacle and The Offerings*. May the Lord be pleased to use it to the blessing of the Lord's people, that there might be a deeper understanding of our Saviour's person and work and a greater devotion to Him.

Ian Jackson
Eastbourne
August, 2018

Contents

Preface 5

Introduction and Outline 9

Chapter 1 17

Chapter 2 33

Chapter 3 67

Chapter 4 91

Chapter 5 113

Introduction and Outline

The writer

The writer of this Epistle is the Apostle John, the last of the New Testament writers. He wrote five New Testament books, all of which were written in the last decade of the first century. These five books are the Gospel according to John, his three Epistles and the book of Revelation.

Purpose in writing

John had different purposes in view when writing his Gospel and his first Epistle. His purpose for writing the Gospel was 'that ye might believe that Jesus is the Christ, the Son of God; and that believing ye might have life through his name', John 20. 31. His purpose for writing the first Epistle was 'that ye may know that ye have eternal life', 1 John 5. 13. In the Gospel, therefore, he writes that we might have eternal life but in the first Epistle he writes that we may know that we have eternal life.

The relation of the Epistle to other books

By comparing the Gospel with the first Epistle it would appear quite conclusive that the Epistle was written subsequent to the Gospel. The prologue of the Gospel, in John chapter 1 verses 1 to 18, sets the background for the opening verses of the Epistle. In the first chapter of his Gospel, John speaks of the Word, life, light and darkness. 'In the beginning was the Word, and the Word was with God, and the Word was God', v. 1. 'In him was life; and the life was the light of men. And the light shineth in darkness; and the darkness comprehended it not', vv. 4, 5. It is with these same thoughts that John opens up his first Epistle. He mentions the Word in verse 1, 'That which was from the beginning, which we have heard, which we have seen with our eyes, which we have looked upon, and our hands have handled, of the Word of life'. He next mentions the life in verse 2, 'For the life was manifested, and we have seen it, and bear witness, and shew unto you that eternal life, which was with the Father, and was manifested unto us'. Then he speaks of light and darkness in verses 6 and 7, 'If we say that we have fellowship with him, and walk in darkness, we lie, and do not the truth: but if we walk in the light, as he is in the light, we have fellowship one with another, and the blood of Jesus Christ his Son cleanseth us from all sin'.

Bringing his Gospel and his Epistles together we can think of them as follows. In his Gospel there is the **pronouncement** of divine truth as John presents to us the basis of all truth, the death and resurrection of our Lord Jesus Christ. Then, in the first Epistle, there is the **practice** of divine truth, the things that ought to be evidenced in the lives of those who profess to know the truth. In the second Epistle there is the **protection** of divine truth; certain deceivers were entered into the world who bring not the doctrine of Christ. These have to be rejected and the doors have to be closed upon them; they are not to be received into our houses nor are we to bid them Godspeed. Then, in the third Epistle John speaks of the **propagation** of divine truth. If in the second Epistle he speaks of deceivers who have entered into the world, in his third Epistle he speaks of those who, for His name's sake, have gone forth taking nothing of the Gentiles. He says that we ought to receive such that we might be fellow-helpers together with the truth. If in the second Epistle we present a closed door so as to protect the truth, in the third Epistle we present an open door in order that the truth might be propagated.

It would also appear that there is a distinct relationship between John's Gospel and the synoptic Gospels. John's ministry is complementary in its character; his Gospel is the complement of the other Gospels, his Epistles are the complement of the other Epistles, and his book of the Revelation is the complement of all earlier prophetic portions in the word of God.

Some general remarks on the Epistle

This Epistle was not written to any particular church or to any particular individual. It is an Epistle that is spoken of as being catholic in its character because it is written for the whole family of God. Seven times in this Epistle, John addresses those to whom he writes as 'little children', a diminutive of affection meaning 'dear children'. The Apostle Paul thinks of God's people as a body in which they are members, Peter thinks of them as a kingdom in which they are subjects, but John thinks of them as a family in which they are children.

John does not deal with salvation from the standpoint of our justification. Rather, the subject of the Epistle is eternal life and the evidences of it, such as love, obedience, boldness and having no fear. Eternal life is a subject not often understood as it ought to be. It is necessary to observe that eternal life was in the Son of God essentially to all eternity. John makes that clear in his Gospel when he says, 'in him was life', John 1. 3. In thinking of eternal life in the Son essentially, it may be thought of as the activity of His own divine nature. It describes that heavenly and eternal condition of relationship or being with the Father. Men speak of their business life, which is life connected with their business, or of their home life, life connected with their home. When it is eternal life that is being considered, it is life that is connected with the Father. Thus, John speaks in his first Epistle of 'that eternal life, which was with the Father, and was manifested unto us', 1. 2. Firstly, then, eternal life was in the Son essentially to all eternity.

Then, it was manifested by the Son at His incarnation. Speaking of the experience of the apostles, John says, 'We have seen it', 1. 2. What a thought it is, however, that that eternal life which was in the Son to all eternity, and manifested at His incarnation, is made available to us through the Son. In the language of the Apostle Paul, Rom. 5. 21, grace is reigning through righteousness unto eternal life, today, through Jesus Christ our Lord. Through Him, and by reason of His work at the place called Calvary, it has been made available to men and women. Eternal life is secured for us in the Son, that Man exalted to God's right hand in heaven. The thought in Romans chapter 6 verse 23 is that the gift of God is eternal life 'in Christ Jesus our Lord' RV. It is 'through' Him, Rom. 5. 21, but it is 'in' Him in chapter 6, secured for us in Him at God's right hand in heaven.

The scriptures tell us how eternal life can be received and who is to receive it. These are important yet very simple matters for any who do not know the Saviour. This eternal life is received by believing in the uplifted Son of man, John 3. 14, 15, believing in the only begotten Son of God, 3. 16 and believing in the Son of the Father's love, 3. 35, 36. In the Son of man uplifted, there is a declaration of God's righteousness; in the only begotten Son who was given, we have a manifestation of God's love; and in the Son of the Father's love, there is the One into whose hands the Father has given all things. The words of the Saviour in John chapter 5 verse 24 are, 'He that heareth my word, and believeth on him that sent me, hath everlasting life'. The word 'on' is italicised; the thought is concerned with believing God's testimony about the Son. John chapter 6 takes it a little further. 'Whoso eateth my flesh, and drinketh my blood, hath eternal life'. This, of course, is certainly not a reference to the breaking of bread, the Lord's supper, but to a personal appropriation of the death of Christ, the means by which we obtain eternal life.

As to who receives eternal life, John tells us in his Gospel 'That whosoever believeth in him should not perish, but have eternal life', 3. 15. It is offered to 'whosoever', each one, anyone and everyone who believes in Him. It is taken further in John chapter 10 verse 28, which tells us that it is sheep who receive it; 'I give unto them eternal life'. There are few things so defenceless as sheep and yet to them He gives eternal life. Again, in John chapter 17 verses 1 and 2, He tells us that He gives eternal life to all who form the Father's love-gift to Him. 'Glorify thy Son, that thy Son may also glorify thee: As thou hast given him power [authority] over all flesh, that he should give eternal life to as many as thou hast given him'.

Division of the book

John's first Epistle is difficult to sectionalize but, broadly speaking, there is a twofold division that can be easily remembered. In the first section, chapters 1 and 2, John speaks of a manifestation and a message. In the second section, chapters 3 to 5, he also speaks of a manifestation and a message.

In chapters 1 and 2, the manifestation is associated with the **person** of the Son. In chapters 3 to 5 the manifestation is associated with the **work** of the Son. In the first section, John speaks of the fact that eternal life was manifested in the person of the Son. The apostles saw it and John testifies concerning it. In the second section, the manifestation is connected with the work of the Son, who 'was manifested to take away our sins', 3. 5 and 'was manifested, that he might destroy the works of the devil', v. 8.

There is also a message found in each section. In the first section, 'This then is the message which we have heard from him . . . that God is light, and in him is no darkness at all', 1. 5. This is a message which was brought by the Son; God is light. In the second section, 'For this is the message that ye heard from the beginning, that we should love one another', 3. 11. (In fact, the expression 'for this' is exactly the same as 'this then', 1. 5.) The message in connection with the second section of the Epistle, therefore, is not a message concerning **light** but a message concerning **love**. It is because of this that we ought to love one another. Accordingly, twice over in this second section John says 'God is love', 4. 8, 16. In summary, and as a broad analysis of the Epistle, in chapters 1 and 2 God is light; in chapters 3 to 5 God is love.

In this Epistle, John presents divine truth in triplets or triads. This is very simple to observe and is an aid to memory. These may be set out as follows.

Life, 1. 1-4

       1.   The manifestation of it.
       2.   The apostolic witness to it
       3.   The apostolic testimony concerning it.

Light, 1. 5 – 2. 2

      A threefold test. 'If we say', vv. 6, 8, 10.

A three-fold test of a man's profession, 2. 3-11

'He that saith', vv. 4, 6, 9.

1. A man's responsibility to God – to obey, vv. 3-5.
2. A man's responsibility to Christ – to follow, vv. 5, 6.
3. A man's responsibility to his brethren – to love, vv. 7-11.

A threefold stage of spirituality in God's family, 2. 12-27

1. Fathers – 'have known him that is from the beginning'.
2. Young men – 'have overcome the wicked one'.
3. Children – 'have known the Father'.

Three manifestations, 2. 28 – 3. 15

1. A future manifestation
    associated with His servants, 2. 28.
    associated with His saints, or His children, 3. 2.
2. A past manifestation
    connected with sins, 3. 5.
    connected with Satan, 3. 8.
3. A present manifestation
    a manifestation of the children of God, 3. 10.
    of the children of the devil, 3. 10.

Three things that we know, 3. 16 – 4. 6

1. A past tense, 3. 16.
    'Herein we have known the love of God'.
2. A future tense, 3. 19
    'And we shall know that we are of the truth'.
3. A present tense, 4. 6
    'Herein we do know the spirit of truth and the spirit of error'.

Three things about the love of God, 4. 7 – 5. 3

    1.   The love of God toward us, 4. 9.
    2.   The love of God perfected in us, 4. 12.
    3.   The love of God made perfect with us, 4. 17.

Three important matters, 5. 4-21

    1.   Faith, vv. 4-13.
              Believing, vv. 5, 10, 13.
    2.   Confidence, vv. 14-17.
              Asking, vv. 14, 15, 16.
    3.   Assurance, vv. 18-21.
              Knowing, vv. 18, 19, 20.

Chapter 1

Life – Chapter 1 verses 1-4

    1.   The manifestation of it, v. 2.
    2.   The apostolic witness to it, v. 2.
    3.   The apostolic testimony concerning it, v. 3.

There is an obvious twofold division in this first chapter that can easily be remembered. In verses 1 to 4 our attention is directed to **a manifestation**, v. 2, whereas in verses 5 to 10 our attention is directed to **a message**, v. 5.

The manifestation, vv. 1-4, is in connection with **life**, 'For the life was manifested, and we have seen it, and bear witness, and show unto you that eternal life, which was with the Father, and was manifested unto us'. In this section, the subject is that of the Father, for 'that eternal life . . . was with the Father', v. 2, and 'our fellowship is with the Father', v. 3. The emphasis in the first section, then, is upon the Father and what is brought before us is the privilege of fellowship that is ours as the people of God. Verse 3 states, 'That which we have seen and heard declare we unto you, that ye also may have fellowship with us'.

The message, vv. 5-10, is connected with **light**. 'This then is the message which we have heard of him, and declare unto you, that God is light, and in him is no darkness at all.' In this section the emphasis is not upon the Father but upon God and the main thought is not that of privilege but of responsibility, connected with the great message that God is light. Three times over in this section there is the expression 'If we say' vv. 6, 8, 10, and in these verses tests are put to us which emphasize the tremendous responsibilities that we have.

In the first section, therefore, there is **the privilege of fellowshipping with the Father** whereas in the second section there is **the responsibility of fellowshipping with God**.
In verses 1 to 4 three matters are predominantly brought before us. Firstly, there is the manifestation of eternal life in a person, the one who

is here spoken of as the Word of Life, the Son of God, v. 2. Secondly, there is the apostolic witness to this manifestation, v. 2. Thirdly, there is the apostolic report of it, v. 3.

1. 1 That which was from the beginning, which we have heard, which we have seen with our eyes, which we have looked upon, and our hands have handled, of the Word of life;

In connection with the manifestation of eternal life in a person, it is interesting to observe that there was given to the apostles a fourfold evidence that Christ was the Word of Life, that He was in His person a manifestation to men of that eternal life which was with, or toward, the Father. Firstly, there was an audible evidence, that 'which we have heard'. Secondly, there was a visible evidence, that 'which we have seen with our eyes'. Then, there was an intelligible evidence, that 'which we have looked upon', or 'contemplated'; and, fourthly, there was tangible evidence, that which 'our hands have handled'.

The expression **'that which was from the beginning'** refers to the beginning of our Lord's public ministry. It is the same in chapter 2 verse 7, where John says, 'Brethren, I write no new commandment unto you, but an old commandment which ye had from the beginning'. The old commandment had been given to them from the beginning of our Lord's public ministry. It is the same expression in Mark chapter 1 verse 1 and Luke chapter 1 verse 2. Luke speaks of certain writers who wrote concerning Christ; they received their details from those who were 'from the beginning eyewitnesses and ministers of the word'. Clearly, this is a reference to the beginning of His public ministry. Of course, in every instance, the expression 'from the beginning' is to be understood in the light of its context, so that it does not necessarily always mean 'from the beginning of His public ministry'. For instance, the reference in chapter 2 verse 24 is to the beginning of the apostolic ministry. Again, John says in chapter 3 verse 8 that 'the devil sinneth from the beginning'; that is, from the beginning of his becoming the devil. The expression is also used in connection with the fathers in chapter 2 verses 13 and 14, where the reference is to the beginning of His public ministry, the details of which we have in the Gospels.

The expression 'in the beginning', John 1. 1, is to be distinguished from 'from the beginning'. In his Gospel, John seems to refer to a 'beginning-less beginning'; as it were, the beginning of eternity.

There seems to be a suggestion too, in the use of the perfect tense in the verbs **'heard'** and **'seen'** that something was heard and seen and continued with them; whereas the verbs **'looked upon'** and **'handled'** are in the point, or aorist tense, something that happened once and for all. 'Heard' and 'seen' would thus refer to His public ministry whereas 'looked upon' and 'handled' refer to certain events associated with His resurrection. In His public ministry, they heard Him and saw His works repeatedly, but, as risen from the dead, they looked upon Him and handled Him. 'Handle me and see', were the words of the Saviour in Luke chapter 24 verse 39.

John begins his Gospel by speaking of Him as the Word; 'In the beginning was the Word', 1. 1, revealing the **heart** of God. In his Epistle, he begins by speaking of Him as **'the Word of Life'**, manifesting the **life** of God. In Revelation, He is 'the Word of God', 19. 13, executing the **judgement** of God. Here, He is the Word of Life; He is revealing the life with the Father.

There were two errors that were prevalent at the time that John wrote. One denied His deity and the other denied the reality of His manhood. In his Gospel, John deals with the first error, which denied His deity, 'In the beginning was the Word, and the Word was with God, and the Word was God'. In his Epistle, however, John deals with the second error, which denied His true manhood, saying that He was not a real man. John says that they know He was a real man; they heard Him, saw Him, contemplated Him and actually handled Him.

1. 2   (For the life was manifested, and we have seen it, and bear witness, and shew unto you that eternal life, which was with the Father, and was manifested unto us;)
John now speaks of the apostolic witness to the manifestation of eternal life. This verse is in brackets because, strictly speaking, it is explanatory

of verse 1. As the Word of life, Christ is simply the manifestation of that eternal life. What the apostles saw was '**the life, the eternal**', as the verse should read. This is an amazing statement; it is not just 'that eternal life' but 'the life, the eternal which was **with the Father**'. In fact, the preposition employed here is 'toward' the Father. This was true to all eternity, but it was manifested here in this world and before the apostles' eyes. Speaking on behalf of the twelve, John says, 'we have seen it'. What a sight for the apostles to behold! The life, the eternal, manifested in a person, here in this world, before their eyes.

The manifestation of the life, the eternal, is therefore much more than a manifestation of the eternity of God's being; it is the manifestation of the life, the eternal, which was toward the Father. It is the quality of life which is toward the Father. 'Toward the Father' is not just 'with' Him as being alongside Him, nor is it 'being with' simply as being a distinct person from the Father. Rather, it is 'toward' the Father involving perpetual movement, perpetual regard and perpetual affection from the Son to the Father. It is this quality of life toward the Father that was manifested here on earth. They saw in a person here on this earth a life which hitherto had only been seen in heaven, the life of the Son toward the Father.

The Son's essential character is a life toward the Father. People speak of their business life (their life in connection with their business), or of their home life (their life in connection with their home) but eternal life is life with, or toward, the Father. That eternal life which was toward the Father, which existed between the Son and the Father to all eternity, was manifested in God's Son here on earth.

It may be summed up like this. John chapters 1 to 7 is the section of that Gospel that deals with life. In chapter 1, it was in Him essentially, for 'in him was life', v. 4. Not only was it in Him essentially but we are told in chapter 3 verse 16 how we receive it, 'whosoever believeth in him should not perish, but have everlasting life'. In chapter 4 verse 14, there is the inward enjoyment of it, for it shall be 'in him a well of water springing up into everlasting life'. In chapter 6 verse 38, it is sustained by feeding on the bread of life, whereas in chapter 7 verse 39 there is the external influence of this life, 'out of his inwards shall flow rivers of living water'.

1. 3   That which we have seen and heard declare we unto you, that ye also may have fellowship with us: and truly our fellowship is with the Father, and with his Son Jesus Christ.

In verse 1 the apostles' **experience** is described. They heard, saw, looked upon and handled and, as has been often pointed out, each statement brings Him nearer. A thing is heard before it is seen and it must be seen before it may be contemplated. It is only then that it may be handled. However, in verse 3 there is not so much their experience but their **testimony** with regard to it, to bring others into the fellowship. 'That which we have seen and heard declare we unto you'; they declared what they had seen of His works and heard of His ministry. In Acts chapter 4 verse 20, Peter says, 'we cannot but speak the things which we have seen and heard'. When it comes to testimony to others, the order is 'seen' and 'heard', the visible before the audible. The same expression occurs again in Acts chapter 22 verse 15, where testimony is in view.

Here, then, there is the report concerning the manifestation of the life, the eternal. The purpose of this apostolic report is **'that ye also may have fellowship with us'** the apostles, whose fellowship is with the Father and with His Son, Jesus Christ.

This **fellowship** can only be enjoyed in the power of the indwelling Holy Spirit. Before the Spirit was given, the apostles were perfectly acquainted with the facts surrounding the Lord's ministry, but their deep meaning was not at that time understood by them. Consider the forty days between His resurrection and His going back to heaven, in which the company of the disciples had received from the Lord the quickening spirit. He said, 'Receive ye the Holy Spirit', John 20. 22, and they entered into an interim enjoyment of things, but the complete realization of the significance of events, prior to and after His death awaited the actual gift of the Holy Spirit. He would bring all these things to their remembrance and impart to them the truth and the meaning of the signs. That is why John says, 'these are written that ye might believe'. John groups them together under the guidance of the Spirit in a way that he could not have done prior to the gift of the Spirit.

In John chapter 20, when the Lord breathed on them and said, 'Receive ye Holy Spirit', it was not **the** Holy Spirit. The Spirit was not given until Jesus was glorified, John 7. 39. What He breathed on them was His own risen life. In Genesis chapter 2, God breathed into man the breath of life; that was natural life, and man became a living soul. But when Jesus breathed on them in John chapter 20 He imparted to them His own risen life, which could only be enjoyed in the power of the Spirit. That is why, in Romans chapter 8, Paul writes of the Spirit of life in Christ Jesus. Life in Christ Jesus, the risen man, is only enjoyed in the power of the Spirit.

Undoubtedly the Spirit of God is guarding the apostles' faithfulness. The reliability of apostolic witness through the Spirit of God is such that nothing can be added to it or taken from it. The report of what the apostles had seen and heard was only given by divine inspiration. The Gospels accurately record what Jesus did and said because the Spirit of God in them brought to their remembrance the things which they had heard and seen. This brings us, who never saw Christ, into the enjoyment of the things which the apostles had already been enjoying. This is the secret of understanding the first four verses.

1. 4   And these things write we unto you, that your joy may be full.

John writes unto them as representing the twelve, **'that your joy may be full'**. The important role of the apostles is thus emphasized. They saw this manifestation of eternal life in the person of the Son of God and they reported this to others who had not seen it. This was so that they might share with the apostles the fellowship that they enjoyed with the Father and with the Son.

John writes that 'your joy may be full', in the sense of them enjoying the things which the apostles have enjoyed. It is just a statement of fact; John is not touching on the conditional side of things, which we have in

John chapter 15. Here, it is the joy of fellowship with the Father and the Son which belongs to every child of God. There might be degrees of joy but John is not thinking of that here. It is fellowship with the Father and the Son. In John chapter 15 verse 11, it is 'my joy' and 'your joy'. His desire was that 'my joy' may become 'your joy' and there are, of course, conditions to that. The joy that is in view in John chapter 15 is Christ's own joy, the joy of an unclouded sky and of uninterrupted communion. He desires that that particular joy of His should become theirs and be always true of them. He never reduces divine truth to our level and always wishes that we could reach the highest level. Therefore, it is clearly conditional. However, in this verse it is the joy that belongs to every child of God.

There are degrees to the joy of fellowship we have with the Father, but John is not treating of that here. Rather, he is treating of what is basic, that which the apostles enjoyed and what they declared, that others might have this particular joy. It is just the joy of being a Christian, the joy of His fellowship. The sharing in common of eternal life involves this fellowship with the Father and fellowship with the Son and sharing with the apostles in that. 'This is life eternal, that they might know thee the only true God, and Jesus Christ. whom thou hast sent', John 17. 3.

The potential of the enjoyment of eternal life involves life, but the actual enjoyment of it involves light.

When John uses **'we'** he is including the other apostles, representatively. In chapter 2 verse 1, he speaks personally; 'I write'. The significant role that the apostles played is not always appreciated. For instance, in Acts chapter 2 verse 42, 'they continued steadfastly in 'the apostles' doctrine and fellowship'. What they had been brought into was fellowship with what the apostles were enjoying. This is basically what we have here; these things are reported that we may be brought into that fellowship that the apostles themselves had been enjoying.

Light – Chapter 1 verse 5 to chapter 2 verse 2

A threefold test.

1. If we say that we have fellowship with him, v. 6
2. If we say that we have no sin, v. 8
3. If we say that we have not sinned, v. 10

In this section John directs our attention to a message that has to do with light. The emphasis is not now on the Father, as in the first section, but upon God. There is also brought before us our responsibility. In connection with this, three professions are brought before us, in verses 6, 8 and 10, in the words, 'if we say'. This is the matter of putting to the test one's profession.

In verses 1 to 4, we have a manifestation concerning the Son; in this section there is a message from the Son. The manifestation concerning the Son involves divine grace, for it was the manifestation of eternal life in the Son. The apostles witnessed this and reported it that we might share with them the fellowship that they enjoyed, fellowship with the Father and with the Son.

In verses 5 to 10 the message from God's Son is not so much connected with divine grace but rather with divine holiness. 'God is light, and in him is no darkness at all'. The manifestation connected with divine grace involved privilege, 'that we may have fellowship', but this message from the Son, declaring God's holiness, involves responsibility. It is necessary to observe that this message that God is light must be never divorced from this manifestation.

1. 5 **This then is the message which we have heard of him, and declare unto you, that God is light, and in him is no darkness at all.**

The expression '**we have heard of him**' does not mean the message they had heard about Him but the message that they had heard from Him. He was not the subject of the message but its source. The message was that '**God is light, and in him is no darkness at all**'. The connection between these first two sections is that in divine grace we have the privilege of fellowship with the Father, vv. 1-4, but the Father remains unchanged as to His nature. He is holy; He is light. Notice also this difference, that in verse 3 John speaks of fellowship with the Father but in verse 6 it is fellowship with God.

The thought of fellowship with the Father and fellowship with God brings John to the burden of the Epistle, which is that Christianity is not just saying, but doing. It is not a matter of mere profession but one of practice.

They heard **the message** from the one who came from the Father, who is 'the eternal life which was with the Father'. He brings to us a message from the Father which the apostles declared unto us. '**Declare**' is almost the same word as 'shew' in verse 2 and 'declare' in verse 3; it means 'to proclaim and to make known', although a prefix is added here which means 'we proclaim it again', that God is light.

John, above all the other writers, does not just write about what God does, or His attributes, but he tells us what God essentially is, unfolding to us the very nature of God. It is John who quotes the words of the Lord, 'God is spirit', John 4. 24; 'God is light', 1 John 1. 5; 'God is love', 4. 8.

'**God is light**' is perhaps a little difficult to define but no figure expresses the thought of purity and perfection so remarkably. Light speaks of brightness, truthfulness, intelligence and untarnished excellence. Possessed with eternal life, sin ought to be hateful to us, for we have fellowship with the Father, who is God and whose nature remains unchanged; God is light. If we have fellowship with such a God, sin must be hateful to us as His children. John adds, '**and in him is no darkness at all**'. This is an important statement, which means that there is nothing shady with our God, never the slightest deviation from what is right, and that is being 'holy'.

'God is light' and 'God is love'. Had there never been a world or a sinner, this is true of God. 'God is'; this is His nature. However, the world was made, man was introduced and evil entered. In a scene of evil, light becomes truth and love becomes grace. 'God is light' and 'God is love' is true of God essentially and eternally; grace and truth are relative terms which relate to the sinner, the unworthy creature of His heart.

1. 6   If we say that we have fellowship with him, and walk in darkness, we lie, and do not the truth:

In this verse and the next verses, there are three professions. In verse 6, '**If we say that we have fellowship with him**' and at the same time we are walking in darkness we are, in fact, bringing God down to our level. In verse 8, 'If we say that we have no sin, we deceive ourselves', thereby elevating ourselves to the divine level. After all, only of our Saviour could it be said truthfully, 'in him is no sin', 3. 5. In verse 10, 'If we say that we have not sinned', there is a Pharisaic profession of super holiness.

The individual in view in verse 6 must be an unbeliever. The believer walks in the light. In the other two professions it may be doubtful whether they are children of God or not, but in the first it is beyond doubt that though he assumes that he has a relationship with God, and is in His family, he is still in darkness.

The **fellowship** here is rather different to the fellowship of the local church. It is the fellowship that embraces all the children of God. Indeed, there is nothing really ecclesiastical in John's first Epistle and thus the fellowship is in relation to the wider sphere of the family of God.

If a person says that he has fellowship with God, he is really saying, 'I am a Christian', because, according to verses 1 and 4, we have fellowship with the Father and with the Son if we have eternal life. This person might say that he has this new relationship with God but John says that if he walks in darkness, just like the unregenerate, being blind to the word of God and spiritual and eternal verities, he lies and does not the truth. Walking in darkness, therefore, refers to our state rather than to our conduct.

Fellowship with the Father and the Son, primarily, is what was enjoyed by the apostles. They reported what they had seen and heard that we might share that fellowship with them. There is also fellowship with God, who is light. This means that we walk as those who are in the light. Then, there is the third fellowship, which we have with one another. If we walk in the light, it is assumed that we are having fellowship with the Father, and, walking in the light, we have fellowship with one another. This is fellowship that embraces all who are in God's family.

It is rather the same idea in 1 Corinthians chapter 1 verse 9, which says, 'God is faithful, by whom ye were called unto the fellowship of his Son Jesus Christ our Lord'. While it is the same fellowship, it is viewed from a different standpoint. Notice, that in 1 Corinthians chapter 1 verse 9, it is not fellowship 'with the Son' but 'the fellowship of his Son'. God's Son, Jesus Christ our Lord, is the bond of the fellowship of Christians. In 1 Corinthians chapter 10 verse 16, we read, 'The cup of blessing which we bless, is it not the communion of the blood of Christ? The bread which we break, is it not the communion of the body of Christ?' Here it is the basis of Christian fellowship that is in view, namely His death, His blood, His body. Then, in 1 Corinthians chapter 16, there is the fellowship of the Holy Spirit, which is the power by which the fellowship is enjoyed.

The word translated **'walk'** here is very interesting. There are two different words for walking in the New Testament. There is in one the thought of walking with deliberate step, used in Acts chapter 21 verse 24 of walking orderly. In the other, which is used here, there is the thought of what is habitual, or 'walking around', one's natural way of going about things. This is not the word describing a soldier marching in step but the bent of one's life. A person is in view who is naturally in a state of darkness. John is not speaking of a lapse but of that which is characteristic of his or her whole life. 'In the light' is positional; walking is our practice in that position.

If we say we have fellowship with God, who is light, but walk in darkness like the unregenerate, **we lie** in our profession and **do not the truth** in our practice. There are, therefore, two matters, profession and practice. Practice is seen in John chapter 3 verse 21, which says, 'He that doeth truth cometh to the light, that his deeds may be made manifest, that they are wrought in God'. 'Do' is a recurring expression in John's first Epistle;

this is the first instance of it. It expresses an action that is continued and repeated, one that is not yet complete.

1. 7 **But if we walk in the light, as he is in the light, we have fellowship one with another, and the blood of Jesus Christ his Son cleanseth us from all sin.**

Walking '**in the light**' is where every child of God walks. There are no degrees of walking in the light, as if some Christians walk more in the light than others; it is not the degree of apprehension of truth that is in view. God is light and He is Himself now 'in the light', which simply means that He is now revealed in the person of His Son. The child of God walks in the light of God having been revealed in the person of His Son.

It is a different thought in Ephesians chapter 5 verse 8, which says that 'ye were sometimes darkness, but now are ye light in the Lord: walk as children of light'. It is our practical Christian living that is in view there but here it is not how we have been walking as children of the light but where we are walking. We walk in the light. If it were the question of our condition, the verse would say, 'If we do not walk in the light, we do not have fellowship one with another and the blood of Jesus Christ his Son, does not cleanse'. This makes it abundantly clear that it is position in view; the grace of God had brought us into the light of God revealed in the person of His Son.

We might have expected John to have said, 'We have fellowship with God' but to walk in the light presupposes this. We cannot walk in the light without having fellowship with God. '**Fellowship one with another**' is not the fellowship of a local church into which we are received and from which we can be put away but it is the fellowship of the family, involving every child of God. Fellowship one with another is the enjoyment of participation in divine life. This is what makes us glad to meet a child of God at any time and to be happy to converse with them over divine things. One may not be free, and rightly so, to associate with unscriptural systems or form unscriptural associations but here it is the family, all who share in this divine life.

We walk in the light, where divine grace has brought us, and the abiding efficacy of '**the blood of Jesus Christ his Son**' keeps us there. This is true of all who are in God's family. To repeat, the abiding efficacy of the blood maintains us in the place into which divine grace has brought us.

The tense of '**cleanseth**' is the present continuous, indicating that it is abiding in its efficacy. There is absolutely no thought, as some would teach, of repeated sprinkling of the blood. The blood of Christ was shed once and for all and the value of that blood reached up to that throne the moment it was shed. It remains before the throne at all times as far as we are concerned. It is the abiding efficacy of the once for all shedding of the blood at the place called Calvary.

If the cleansing is not in respect of every sin then it is not in respect of any sin. It surely rejoices our hearts that the blood of Jesus cleanses us from all sin, every sin and any sin. God loves the sinner but He saves because of His own estimate and appreciation of the blood.

1. 8   If we say that we have no sin, we deceive ourselves, and the truth is not in us.

If, in verse 6, a person is having low thoughts about God he now has high thoughts about self. '**Sin**' is in the singular; John is speaking of sin as an evil principle, of what we might term 'inherent' sin. Of only one could it be said, 'in him is no sin', 3. 5; but here is a person who says he is different from all others in having no sin.

If we say this **we deceive ourselves**. This is an important expression. In chapter 3 verse 7, John says, 'Little children, let no man deceive you' but here is a deception of their own making. The meaning of the word is, 'we are leading ourselves astray'. It is a strong word and involves a serious condition.

Not only are we leading ourselves astray if we say this but **the truth is not in us**. It is not here disbelief of the truth, nor is it ignorance of the truth, but that the truth has never had its rightful place in me.

The teaching of God's word in this matter is very interesting and important to observe. Paul teaches in Romans chapter 7 that sin dwells in every Christian. He says, in verse 17, 'Now then it is no more I that do it, but sin that dwelleth in me'. That does not mean, of course, that we should serve sin. In Romans chapter 6 verse 6, the apostle says, 'Knowing this, that our old man is crucified with him, that the body of sin might be destroyed, that henceforth we should not serve sin'. Notice, though, the change of language when it comes to Christ. Paul says in Galatians chapter 2 verse 20, 'I am crucified with Christ: nevertheless I live; yet not I, but Christ liveth in me'. Sin 'dwelleth in me' but 'Christ liveth in me'. It does not say 'sin liveth in me'; it dwells there but we should not serve it.

1. 9   If we confess our sins, he is faithful and just to forgive us our sins, and to cleanse us from all unrighteousness.

There is a change of language here. Verse 8 says, 'If we say' but verse 9 says, '**If we confess**'. It is not now profession in view; John has before him the individual who is obviously a real Christian. In verse 8, in high sounding profession, there is evidently no self-judgement. In verse 9, however, there is sincere confession as a result of self-judgement; it is humble contrition.

The moment I put my trust in Christ all the sins that could be associated with my name were judicially forgiven by a holy God. They are never again to be remembered. In chapter 2 verse 12, John says, 'I write unto you, little children, because your sins are forgiven you for his name's sake'. However, in this verse, it is the Father who forgives. This is not God's judicial forgiveness but forgiveness within the circle of the family, a Father's forgiveness. These are two different matters. God's forgiveness has to do with our conscience; it is judicial, once and for all, and, because of that, Hebrews chapter 10 speaks of having no more conscience of sins. But the Father's forgiveness, which is not connected to conscience, is connected with the restoration of communion.

We shall observe in chapter 2 that John says, 'these things write I unto you, that ye sin not'. These things are not written to give us licence to sin but so that we should not sin.

'Confession' is a compound of two Greek words, meaning to 'speak together'. It is agreeing with another and, thus, the idea of confessing sin means that I agree with God about it, seeing my sin as He sees it. It is not a matter of concealing sin or consoling ourselves with regard to sin; we must never do that. Rather, it is a matter of confessing our sins, something which is very important to do.

Confession is specific, meaning I tell God the Father exactly what I have done. I feel that we would be all better Christians if we not only understood this but endeavoured to put it into practice. Confession ought always to be made under the shadow of the cross, recognizing that it was for that very sin the Saviour suffered as He did. If it grips our hearts that for that very sin His blood was shed we will not turn to the same sin again.

Confession brings us into the good of a forgiveness that is awaiting us. It awaits us because of the blood, but it is only enjoyed by us in the moment we confess.

'**He is faithful and just**'. One would have thought that John would have said that He is 'merciful and gracious to forgive us' but he says 'faithful and just to forgive us'. He is faithful to the blood, and just because of it, to grant us this forgiveness.

He is faithful and just **to forgive** us our sins and **to cleanse** us from all unrighteousness. The idea is that He forgives the act and He cleanses from the resultant state. **Sins** lead to **unrighteousness**, which results in a lack of integrity, but if we confess our sins He forgives the sinful acts and cleanses us from the resulting unrighteousness state.

This cleansing is not cleansing by the blood but by the word. He does not **cleanse** us by convicting us, for the period of conviction is past, but, confession having been made, the Father cleanses us by giving us the assurance from His word of the abiding efficacy and cleansing power of the blood.

1. 10   If we say that we have not sinned, we make him a liar, and his word is not in us.

'**If we say that we have not sinned**' means 'if we say we have not committed sinful acts'. This is different to verse 8, which says, 'If we say that we have no sin'. The difference is that if we say that we have no sin it is reference to that which is inward but if we say that we have not sinned the reference is to outward sinful acts. The professor in verse 8 says that the evil principle is not in him but in verse 10 he says that whilst it is in him it has never exerted itself.

If we say that we have not sinned **we make God a liar**. In verse 8, we deceive ourselves; self-deception is bad enough, but here we make God a liar. The veracity of God is attacked and this is much more serious. The word 'make' is a strong word. It is the same word that occurs in John chapter 19 verse 7, in 'he made himself the Son of God'. God has said in His word, in Romans chapter 3 verse 23, that 'all have sinned' and for anyone to say that he is an exception makes God a liar; the truthfulness of God and of His word is attacked. Also, if God promises forgiveness then to say that I have not sinned attacks His truthfulness again.

In verse 8, the truth is not in us; in verse 10, His word is not in us. 'Truth', in verse 8, is a general statement; divine truth, in a general sense, is not in us. This involves disbelief of the truth and rejection of it. However, 'his word' is not in us, in verse 10, as it relates to the case in point; God's word says that He cannot lie.[1]

---

[1] Num. 23. 19; 1 Sam. 15. 29; Titus 1. 2; Heb. 6. 18.

Chapter 2

2. 1 My little children, these things write I unto you, that ye sin not. And if any man sin, we have an advocate with the Father, Jesus Christ the righteous:

Verses 1 and 2 are a supplement to chapter 1. They contain God's provision for the child of God, should he sin. There are seven statements to consider in these two verses.

'My little children' occurs seven times in John's first Epistle and once in his Gospel. It is not a diminutive that is to do with age, such as occurs later in the chapter, but a diminutive which speaks of affection. It is sometimes rendered 'my dear children' and includes all in God's family; the infants, the young men, and the fathers.

It is necessary to observe how John thinks of those to whom he is writing. He is thinking of them as children, belonging to a family, being not just precious to the heart of God but to John's heart as well. One could wish that speaking of them with affection, as we ought, would be more characteristic of us today.

'These things write I unto you'. The things to which John refers are those matters he ministered about in chapter 1, in which he has spoken to them of a manifestation of life and a message concerning light; privilege and responsibility.

'That ye sin not'. The great complaint of the moralist today is that if the blood of Jesus Christ His Son cleanses us from all sin we can sin as we wish. However, John has written of the abiding efficacy of the blood and of a Father's forgiveness not to give a licence to sin but 'that ye sin not'. Remember, God is love and God is light.

'If any man sin'. The preceding statement is 'that ye sin not' but John now changes the language. He does not say 'if ye sin' but 'if any man', or anyone, 'sin'. It should not be thought that John is referring to those who are outside of God's family; rather, it is 'if any one of God's family sin'. If

John had said if 'ye' sin, he would have addressed himself to the whole family, which would have indicated that to sin was common in the family of God. By the change in language he carefully avoids indicating that this is something that is characteristic of God's family.

John might have used the future tense, 'If any man shall sin' but that would make us think that John is making provision for one who is intending to sin. He might also have used the present tense, 'If any man sins' but that would have the thought of character, what is continuous or habitual. In fact, he uses the aorist which never indicates a course that is pursued or something that is habitual; it indicates a definite act. What John has in mind here is the child of God falling into a single sin.

'**We have an advocate with the Father**'. Here is another remarkable change in language. It is not ye or any man but 'we' have an advocate. This is something that is true of all of us, as true as is our possession of eternal life and our justification. We have this advocate at all times whether we realize it or not and whether we sin or not.

Our advocate is '**with the Father**', which is a beautiful truth. The priesthood of Christ is in relation to God. Hebrews chapter 2 verse 17 says, 'Wherefore in all things it behoved him to be made like unto his brethren, that he might be a merciful and faithful high priest in things pertaining to God, to make reconciliation for the sins of the people'. Our advocate, however, is not 'with God' but 'with the Father'. That means, at least, that even if I sin God still remains my Father. Not just **my** Father, nor **His** Father but **the** Father. He is the Father of His own Son and my Father too. Thus, there is absolutely no thought anywhere in the scripture of a 'fall away' doctrine. Once I am in the family of God I am there forever. God remains my Father, for nothing can dissolve this relationship; I remain, always, a child in the family.

The word 'advocate' is *parakletos*. '*Para*' means alongside of; *kaléō* means 'to call'. Thus, an advocate is 'one who is called alongside of'. It is the same word used of the Comforter in John's Gospel, who is called alongside to teach and to convict. 'We have an advocate with the Father' involves two things. Two prepositions are employed here. He is 'with' (*pros*) or 'towards', the Father; and the word *parakletos* has the preposition *para*, which means 'along with'. As our advocate, He is therefore towards the Father and comes alongside us. He is not called alongside the Father; He is toward Him. In chapter 1 verse 2, He is that eternal life which was towards the Father; in John chapter 1 verse 1 He is the Word who was towards God.

What John is emphasizing here is that He is now back in the place from whence He came, which is 'towards the Father'. With regard to the child of God, however, He is called alongside as an advocate. He comes alongside the child who has sinned, firstly to make the child of God, if necessary, aware of a sin that has been committed; and, secondly, to convict them of the wrong of that sin and bring him to the point of confession. It is only then that forgiveness is experienced and enjoyed. The prepositions make all this clear. Thus, His advocacy involves the fact that sin has disturbed communion with the Father and He acts so that that communion is restored.

It is a comfort to know that we have such an advocate, but His ministry is convicting rather than comforting.

This advocate, as to his person, is '**Jesus Christ the righteous**'. It is important that our advocate is righteous; it means that when He deals with the sin we have committed He deals faithfully and righteously with every sin, and that to the glory of God the Father.

2.2   And he is the propitiation for our sins: and not for ours only, but also for the sins of the whole world.

Having spoken of His person, John now speaks of His work. As to His person, He is righteous in His character and, as to His work. He has righteously expiated sin, and is in the presence of God in all the value of the sacrifice of Calvary

He is the propitiation on the throne. The work of propitiation was accomplished by Him at Calvary as the propitiator, but He lives on the throne as the propitiation to make good to us the work that He accomplished at Calvary.

In Romans chapter 3 verse 25, the apostle states that God has set Him forth as a propitiation, a word which has the thought of Him being the meeting place for God and man based on the propitiatory work accomplished at Calvary.

There has been a great deal of play on the omission of the words 'the sins of' in the original text. Because of this omission some say that He is not the propitiation for **the sins of the whole world**, but He is, and we do well to remember that. Though the words are italicized, they are grammatically and necessarily understood. Propitiation is not in relation to persons or the world but always has to do with sins.

In view of those who make much of the fact that the words 'the sins of' are in italics, Hebrews chapter 7 verse 27 should be considered. It says, 'Who needeth not daily, as those high priests, to offer up sacrifice, first for his own sins, and then for the people's; for this he did once, when he offered up himself'. 'Sins' is not mentioned the second time there, but, as in this verse, it is understood. It is the very same grammatical setting.

Propitiation is always Godward and it must be remembered that the blood of Christ, and His sacrifice, was greater than the throne of God demanded. The sacrifice of Christ, the blood of Christ, is infinite in its value. In its Godward aspect, it satisfied God's throne in respect of its demands, not in relation to our sins only but in relation to the sins of the whole world. If there never had been one soul saved, God had been infinitely satisfied and glory brought to His name in respect of the sins of the whole world.

Propitiation is not the removal of God's judgement, as those who do not avail themselves of it still come under the judgement of God, but it is the removal of God's displeasure in the sense that Paul can now say that God 'will have all men to be saved'. God's pleasure now is in the matter of salvation because of the propitiatory sacrifice.

Propitiation is far more than appeasement. There is no such thing as appeasement with God. God needs not to be appeased. In fact, propitiation does not alter God one bit; God is unchanging in His love and in His righteousness. Propitiation satisfies His just demands in relation to sins. When we think of appeasement, it is in relation to an irate or angry person.

What we enjoy, the result of propitiation having been made, is the judicial forgiveness of a holy God, which is once for all. What we enjoy upon confession of our sin is not the forgiveness of a holy God but the forgiveness of the Father; it is forgiveness within the circle of the family, for us as children. These are two different matters.

A three-fold test of a man's profession, vv. 3-11

'He that saith', vv. 4, 6, 9.

1. A man's responsibility to God – to obey, vv. 3-5.
2. A man's responsibility to Christ – to follow, vv. 5-6.
3. A man's responsibility to his brethren – to love, vv. 7-11.

John now wants to apply this threefold test of profession. Responsibility to God means obedience to His word; responsibility to Christ involves indebtedness to follow Him; responsibility to the brethren involves loving them.

2. 3   And hereby we do know that we know him, if we keep his commandments.

In verses 3 to 5 there is brought before us the first test and it is relation to a man's responsibility to God, which is obedience to His word. In verse 3 there is the genuine child of God, but in verse 4 there is the empty and false profession of one who is content, and perhaps proud, to claim that he is a Christian.

'Hereby' or 'herein' **'we do know'** is in the present tense, speaking of a present knowledge. This is based on a past experience, the expression '**we know him**' being in the perfect tense, which has the significance 'we have known him'. We have this continuing knowledge that we have come to know Him '**if we keep his commandments**'. Here is a very important matter; obedience is not optional but is a necessary evidence of a vital knowledge of God.

To obey His commandments involves the exercise of the will. In chapter 3 verse 23, John says, 'And this is his commandment, that we should believe on the name of his Son Jesus Christ, and love one another, as he gave us commandment'. This is primarily the commandment to which John refers in this verse, whereas the 'commandments' referred to in John chapter 14 verse 15, in the expression, 'If ye love me, keep my commandments', are more general than in his Epistle. John specifies his commandment and it is that we believe and love. Obedience is not to be selective, obeying what merely suits, but it is to be unqualified. This is one of the tests that gives us assurance.

The idea of 'knowing' is characteristic of John's Epistle. The subject matter of this book is life; 'and this is life eternal, that they might know thee the only true God, and Jesus Christ, whom thou hast sent', John 17. 3. Life eternal is knowledge; to know God and to know the Son.

2. 4   He that saith, I know him, and keepeth not his commandments, is a liar, and the truth is not in him.

'**I know him**' is in the past tense and refers to the professor. '**Keepeth not**' is in the present continuous. The idea in the verse, therefore, is that the person who says, 'I have known him' but does not continually keep His commandments is a liar in word and the truth is not in him in his practice.

2. 5   But whoso keepeth his word, in him verily is the love of God perfected: hereby know we that we are in him.

By way of contrast to verse 4, this verse refers to the child of God. '**Whoso keepeth his word**'. It is not now 'his commandments' but 'his word'. It is not now keeping an explicit commandment, which involves subjection to divine authority, but keeping His word, as it unfolds to us His will. This involves being captivated by the preciousness of His word and the preciousness of His will as revealed in it.

With regard to all such, John says, '**in him verily is the love of God perfected**'. This means that the love of God in him reaches its desired end, which is that it might be returned in our genuine love to God.

2. 6   He that saith he abideth in him ought himself also so to walk, even as he walked.

The second test, in verse 6, is in relation to my responsibility to Christ. It is a debt to follow his example, '**to walk, even as he walked**'. In chapter 1 verse 7, it is walking in the light of God revealed in the person of His Son in the matter of salvation, but here it is the idea of following His example. A profession of abiding in Him is negated if we are not walking as He walked.

This section really begins in the last part of the verse 5, 'hereby we know that we are in him'. In verse 3, it is 'we do know that we know him' but now it is rather different, knowing 'that we are in him'. Against the background of the child of God having this inward knowledge of being in Christ, there is, in verse 6, the profession of abiding in Christ.

In the previous section, verses 3 to 5, John has been teaching that disobedience makes false any profession of a past experience; I have not known him if I am disobedient. Verse 6, however, teaches that indifference to the example set before us in Christ makes false any profession of a present experience: 'He that saith he abideth'. If a person belongs to Christ, he shall never be indifferent to His example; he shall always seek to discharge the debt of endeavouring to walk as He walked.

Notice that verse 5 says, 'we know that we are in him', but when it comes to the professor, in verse 6, he goes further than saying 'I am in Him'; it is, '**he that saith he abideth in him**'. Abiding in Him is dwelling in Him; it simply means that Christ is my home, that I cleave to Him, dwell with him and enjoy Him in every vicissitude of life. This is not possible if there is unconfessed sin in the life.

'**In him**' in John's Epistle is somewhat different from 'in him' in the Pauline Epistles. In the Pauline Epistles it is the thought of security, such as, for instance in Romans chapter 8 verse 1, 'There is therefore now no condemnation to them which are in Christ Jesus'. John takes up the idea of 'in him' from a different standpoint. The Lord Jesus said in John chapter 14 verse 20, 'At that day ye shall know that I am in my Father, and ye in me, and I in you'. This is not so much the thought of security but of being in the enjoyment of the Son's love even as He was in the enjoyment of the Father's love and the Father was in the enjoyment of the love of the Son.

John uses strong words here. The word '**ought**' involves a debt to pay. The word occurs in chapter 3 verse 16, 'we ought to lay down our lives for the brethren'; in chapter 4 verse 11, 'we ought also to love one another'; in 3 John verse 8, we 'ought to receive such'.

It is very interesting to observe that John, who says that we ought **to walk even as He walked**, is the one who speaks repeatedly in his Gospel of the walk of Christ. In fact, it makes a lovely subject to study. In John chapter 1 verse 35, John the Baptist, standing with two of his disciples, looked 'upon Jesus as he walked' and said, 'Behold the Lamb of God'. In chapter 7 verse 1, He 'walked in Galilee', the place of reproach. In chapter 10 verse 23, it was winter and 'Jesus walked in the temple in Solomon's porch'. In chapter 11 verse 54, He 'walked no more openly'.

We could not stand with John, or walk in Galilee, or in Solomon's porch in the temple, and so there is a spiritual aspect to the walk as far as we are concerned. In chapter 1, there was that about His walk that marked him out as the Lamb of God. Paul thinks of this when he says in 2 Corinthians chapter 10 verse 1, that he was beseeching them 'by the meekness and gentleness of Christ'; it is walking in meekness, as He walked. In chapter 7, the Son of God from heaven walked in Galilee, the place of reproach; we, too, are to walk with Him in the place of His reproach, Heb. 13. 13. In chapter 10, He walked not in the temple but in Solomon's porch, that which spoke of the pristine glory of the temple; we walk there by strengthening the things that remain. In chapter 11, He walked no more openly because of the Jews; when He deemed it necessary, He was prepared to withdraw from public life, something the flesh can never do.

In 1 Peter chapter 2 verse 21, following in His steps relates to His example of suffering for righteousness' sake. Peter has in view the domestic servant being buffeted for doing well. In 1 Corinthians chapter 11 verse 1, Paul says, 'Be ye followers of me, even as I also am of Christ'. John says, here, that we ought to walk as He walked.

2. 7   Brethren, I write no new commandment unto you, but an old commandment which ye had from the beginning. The old commandment is the word which ye have heard from the beginning.

In verses 7 to 11, the third test of profession is in relation to our responsibility to our brethren, which is to love them, vv. 9-10. These are difficult verses.

'**Brethren**' is really the word 'beloved'. '**From the beginning**' is the beginning of Christ's ministry, of which they had heard. Christ gave it when He was here and they had heard it from the apostles. The second occurrence of the words 'from the beginning' are omitted as John is, of course, writing to people who had not heard it from the beginning. Thus, the verse reads, 'Beloved, I write no new commandment unto you, but an old commandment which ye had from the beginning. The old commandment is the word which ye have heard'.

The **old commandment** had been handed down to them. They had heard it from the apostles, that they had to love as Christ Himself loved. It is not the commandment given under the law. Rather, the commandment was old in the sense that it began with Christ when He was here but it was new in their experience.

2. 8   Again, a new commandment I write unto you, which thing is true in him and in you: because the darkness is past, and the true light now shineth.

There is an apparent contradiction between verses 7 and 8, as John now says, '**Again, a new commandment I write unto you**'. It was '**true in him**'; Christ loved, and said that they were to love one another 'as I have loved you', John 13. 34. This was not only true in Christ but also in those to whom John was writing, '**and in you**'. Now that Christ has gone to heaven, and the Holy Spirit has come, it is true 'in you'.

It was not true in the apostolic band when the Christ was here because they were still on the ground of the law, commanded to love their neighbour as they love themselves. But now, says John, it is true in you **because the darkness is passed** (or, more accurately, 'is passing') **and the true light now shineth** (or, 'the true light is already shining'). The darkness is passing, not in terms of a believer's experience but as far as the world is concerned. He loved but He was put to death; but that darkness of His rejection and crucifixion is now passing as the love that was displayed in Him is now displayed in us.

It must be remembered that the new commandment is to love. The darkness here is not the darkness that characterized the Old Testament, but the darkness caused by the rejection of the one in whom it was true. The true light was already shining; the true light is connected with the new commandment and was already being exhibited in those who had put their trust in Him.

2. 9   He that saith he is in the light, and hateth his brother, is in darkness even until now.

Against this we have the proud professor, 'He that saith he is in the light'. No true child of God goes around saying, 'I am in the light' but empty professors are usually very bold, being guilty not only of profession but of high-sounding profession. Of course, every true child of God is in the light, as was seen in chapter 1.

No matter what he professes, however, the one who continually **hateth his brother is in darkness until now**, meaning that even though the true light is now shining he remains in his unregenerate state; he has never been born again. As we proceed in this Epistle we shall see how important it is to observe the tenses of the verbs. '**He that hateth**' is in the present continuous; he who hates continually and habitually. It does not relate to an isolated instance or instances, but it is the unaltered character of the individual that is in view. Of course, that is very solemn. If there is a continual, unabated hatred towards a Christian and this is what characterizes me then I might well question if I have ever been born of God at all!

Some wonder at the expression 'hateth his brother', but when it comes to the mere professor. the word 'brother' is an assumed relationship, rather than a vital one.

2. 10   He that loveth his brother abideth in the light, and there is none occasion of stumbling in him.

He that loveth his brother continually, despite every trial that might militate against it, abideth in the light. Notice that it does not say that 'he is in the light' or 'he that walks in the light'. Notice the accuracy of the word of God; it says, 'abideth in the light', meaning that the light has become his home.

'**There is none occasion of stumbling in him**' means that there is nothing in him that would cause another to stumble. This is very important; he will never seek revenge or feel satisfied when someone is hurt or injured. These are the things that mark the true believer.

2. 11   But he that hateth his brother is in darkness, and walketh in darkness, and knoweth not whither he goeth, because that darkness hath blinded his eyes.

Again, in the expression '**hateth his brother**', 'brother' is only an assumed relationship; and 'hateth' being in the present continuous it is his character that is in view. He '**is in darkness**'. The article is used, meaning that the reference is to 'the darkness', showing it to be the darkness of the unregenerate state where there is no light of salvation. He '**knoweth not whither he goeth**', which is to perdition, because that '**darkness hath blinded his eyes**'. The darkness of his profession has blinded his eyes as to his destiny, and so he is not only in the darkness but he '**walketh in darkness**'; he could not do otherwise.

A threefold stage of spirituality in God's family, vv. 12-27

Three stages in the family of God.

1. Fathers.
2. Young men.
3. Infants.

When John says, in verse 12, 'I write unto you, little children', it is the same expression as he uses in verse 1 and verse 28. 'Little children' in each of these verses refers to all, without distinction, who are in the family of God. However, when the apostle says 'Little children' in verses 13 and 18 he employs a different word, which refers to a certain class in God's family. It is a word which means 'infants'. Unless we make this distinction, we shall never understand these verses properly.

There are three classes in God's family and John writes twice to each class. The three stages in the family of God are fathers, young men and children. He writes to the fathers twice, in verses 13 and 14. He then writes to the young men in verse 13 and verses 14 to 17. Then, towards the end of verse 13, he addresses the infants, and again in verses 18 to 27. This is a long section and it is often not understood that he is addressing the infants throughout.

2. 12   I write unto you, little children, because your sins are forgiven you for his name's sake.

'**Little children**' is a diminutive of affection, not of age, which is sometimes therefore rendered 'dear children'. Age makes distinction but affection rules out distinction. It occurs seven times in the Epistle.[2] On each occasion, it embraces all who are in God's family. It makes an interesting study to observe what John says of the dear children of God's family.

The word for 'little children' is a diminutive of the word for 'child'. John actually uses three words. He uses 'children', which means born ones and 'infants', in verse 13, which is a diminutive of age, making distinction in God's family. In verse 12, he uses 'dear children' or 'beloved children'. This word occurs once in John's Gospel, in chapter 13 verse 33, where the Lord says, 'Little children, yet a little while I am with you'. It bespeaks His great love towards them.

Of each dear child in the family of God John says, **'your sins are forgiven you for his name's sake'**. How delightful! He does not say he is writing to them that they might know that their sins are forgiven but because their sins are forgiven them. Notice 'your sins'. It is a plenary forgiveness, being not in respect of just some sins but all of them, whether they be great or small, many or few.

They are forgiven them **'for his name's sake'**. The idea of 'His name' supposes His absence, but there is more to it than that. The 'name' stands for all that Christ is and all that He has done. It is wonderful to think that we enjoy plenary forgiveness of sins as a present possession because of all that Christ is and all that Christ has done. Ephesians chapter 4 verse 32 should read, 'even as God in Christ hath forgiven you'. Forgiveness 'for his name's sake' is how John puts it; forgiveness by 'God in Christ' is how Paul puts it.

2. 13   I write unto you, fathers, because ye have known him that is from the beginning. I write unto you, young men, because ye have overcome the wicked one. I write unto you, little children, because ye have known the Father.

---

[2] See: 2. 1, 12, 28; 3. 7, 18; 4. 4; 5. 21.

John now writes to the fathers, who are the most mature in God's family. The fathers had **known him that is from the beginning**, that is Christ. The fathers had this knowledge of Christ as having been made known to men from the beginning of His public ministry, from the beginning of His having been made known to men. It is to be observed that this is what John says to the fathers, the spiritually mature. A personal, intimate knowledge of Christ is the high-water level of Christian experience, the mark of spiritual maturity. There can be nothing higher as far as spiritual experience is concerned.

John next writes to the **young men**. They are marked by spiritual vigour, which has been evidenced by their overcoming the **wicked one**, the evil one. John mentions the evil one on another two occasions in his Epistle, at chapter 3 verse 12 and chapter 5 verse 18. The young men had overcome not the flesh, nor the world but the evil one.

Now John addresses himself to the **little children**, the infants. The fathers know Christ, the young men know the power of the evil one, but the infants in God's family know the Father. To know the Father is the birthright of the youngest, the most immature in the family of God. Peter says, 'And if ye call on the Father', 1 Peter 1. 17, which has the significance of, 'if ye invoke God as Father'.

This is something unique to the day in which we live. The nation of Israel knew something of God as Father. In Malachi chapter 1 verse 6, He says, 'if then I be a father, where is mine honour?' In Exodus chapter 4 verse 22, He says of Israel, 'Israel is my son'. However, sonship did not belong to the Israelites individually; they were God's son as a nation and He was their Father nationally. In Romans chapter 9 verse 4, Paul says, 'to whom pertaineth the adoption' or 'sonship', as a nation. In contrast, what belongs to the day in which we live is that the most immature, the most inexperienced, child of God knows God as Father.

There is today an increase in addressing God in prayer as 'the Almighty' and so on. Let us remember that we know God in a much more intimate way than as 'the Almighty'. We know him in a way that nobody else has ever known Him, for we know him individually as 'Father'. Perhaps we remember the joy that flooded our heart when, after we had been saved, for the first time meaningfully and truthfully in prayer we could say, 'Father, Father'.

'Heavenly Father' is the language of an earthly people. The expression 'heavenly Father' never occurs outside of the Gospels. When we address God, we address Him as Father, the God and Father of our Lord Jesus Christ. We have to be careful in dealing with those, perhaps younger people, who address God as 'heavenly Father' that we do not stumble them but lead them on to a greater appreciation that we are not an earthly people who stand in relation to a heavenly Father. In this day, we stand in relation to the Father of our Lord Jesus Christ.

In Galatians chapter 4 verse 6, 'God hath sent forth the Spirit of his Son into your hearts, crying, Abba, Father'. Observe that He is not called 'the Spirit of God' but the 'Spirit of his Son'. This brings us in a very real way into relationship with God as Father. The Spirit of God in us is the Spirit of His Son. In Romans chapter 8 verse 15, it is the children who say 'Abba, Father', whereas, in Galatians chapter 4 verse 6, it is the Spirit of his Son who cries 'Abba, Father'. The two are thus brought together; His Spirit witnesses with our spirit that we are the children of God.

It is remarkable to observe that 'Abba, Father' was the language of God's Son in the garden of Gethsemane, Mark 14. 36; and wonderful to think that sinners saved by grace can address God in the same way as did His Son. We can do this because of the Spirit of His Son sent into our hearts. In Romans chapter 3, the poison of asps was under our lips, our throats were an open sepulchre, but, saved by wondrous grace, we now employ the same language as the Son Himself, 'Abba, Father'.

'Abba' is the Aramaic for 'father'. There are a number of reasons why the word 'Abba' is used. Firstly, some say that this is just the infant saying 'papa', but we would be wrong to think this. It is not the lisping of an infant but, rather, the heart cry of a son, as is evident in the garden of Gethsemane. Secondly, 'Abba' is the Aramaic, 'Father' is the Greek. Therefore, it embraces both Jew and Gentile. Thirdly, whenever there is untranslated Aramaic in the New Testament it always implies deep pathos and feeling. Examples of this are 'Eloi, Eloi, lama sabachthani?' Mark 15. 34, and 'Anathema. Maranatha', 1 Cor. 16. 22.

2. 14 **I have written unto you, fathers, because ye have known him that is from the beginning. I have written unto you, young men, because ye are strong, and the word of God abideth in you, and ye have overcome the wicked one.**

John now writes for the second time to the **fathers**. The important point to observe here is that when he writes the second time to the fathers he repeats what he had said to them the first time. He makes no additions, for the simple reason that nothing can be added to a person having a personal, intimate knowledge of Christ; there is nothing higher in spiritual experience.

Then, in verses 14 to 17, he writes to the **young men** for the second time and there are certain additions to what he said before. The additions indicate that the secret of their strength in overcoming the evil one was that the word of God was abiding in them. It is not simply that these young men knew the word of God; although it is necessary to know it, mere knowledge is not the source of strength. In fact, it is possible to know the word of God and be very weak. John says that they were strong because the word of God had an abiding place in their hearts and lives.

2. 15 **Love not the world, neither the things that are in the world. If any man love the world, the love of the Father is not in him.**

He now gives to the young men a warning in relation to the world. '**Love not the world**'. No such warning was given to the fathers, because the world has no appeal to those who intimately know Christ. To these vigorous young men, however, there can be the appeal of the world.

There are four words in the Greek New Testament that help us to understand the significance of '**the world**'. The word *ge* is used for the earth, as distinguished from the heavens. The word *oikoumene* is used for the inhabited world, the world of men. The word *aion* relates to an age, or a generation, or the conditions that pertain in any particular epoch of man's history. There is also the word *kosmos*, which is used here.

Kosmos, which carries the idea of order and arrangement, occurs in different senses throughout the New Testament. In John chapter 1 verse 10, it says, 'He was in the world, and the world was made by him, and the world knew him not'. The word *kosmos* is repeated in that verse but it obviously has more than one significance. 'He was in the world' that He made; 'the world' of humanity 'knew him not'. *Kosmos* is used of the universe, of the human race and of human life in its alienation from God.

In John chapter 3 verse 16, God loved the world of humanity with a view to its salvation. We, too, ought to have the love of God in us as far as the world of humanity is concerned, and be desirous of the salvation of our fellow men. However, John is speaking here of the world morally, of human life as a system in which people are happy to be estranged from God.

It is possible to be strong by means of the word of God abiding in us and yet the world can still have an appeal, and so John says to these young men, 'Love not the world'. Sometimes, brethren who have advanced spiritually through the word of God abiding in them and have overcome the evil one, have succumbed to the things of the world. In 2 Timothy chapter 4 verse 10, Demas loved this present *aion*, the age in which he lived, evil in its character, something to which, in Romans chapter 12 verse 2, the Christian is not to be conformed.

There is a contrast between the world and the Father in both verses 15 and 16. In the words of the Son of God in John chapter 17 verse 25, when He said, 'O righteous Father, the world hath not known thee: but I have known thee', the sharp distinction between the Father and the world is clearly seen. '**The love of the Father is not in him**' does not mean that the Father has stopped loving him; rather, by loving the world he has withdrawn himself from the enjoyment of that love. We cannot at the same time love the world and have the enjoyed, daily experience of the love of the Father being in us. Of course, you do not cease to be a child of God if the love of the Father is not in you; you do not move out of the light into the darkness if you love the world, but the love of the Father is not an enjoyed portion.

2. 16 **For all that is in the world, the lust of the flesh, and the lust of the eyes, and the pride of life, is not of the Father, but is of the world.**

All that is in the world is out of the world; it has its source in the world. All that is in the world is spoken of as being the lust of the flesh, the lust of the eyes, and the pride of life. These do not have their source in the Father and thus the world bears no likeness to Him whatsoever. These, then, are not necessarily material objects, though these can be a snare. The context would suggest that what John has in mind are the evil motives and principles that operate in the world of men estranged from God.

The **lust of the flesh** originates in the flesh and produces desires for sensual pleasures. The **lust of the eyes** is lust which originates in what we see and has to do with the satisfaction, visually, of sinful pleasure. The Lord Jesus warned against this in Matthew chapter 5 verse 28: 'whosoever looketh on a woman to lust after her hath committed adultery with her already in his heart'.

The **pride of life** is the boasting of life. 'Life' occurs again in chapter 3 verse 17, where John speaks of one who has this world's 'good', this world's means or subsistence. It is, therefore, the matter of boasting in one's accumulation of worldly goods. This does not have its origin with the Father but in the world.

The lust of the flesh and the lust of the eyes can be private sins that nobody knows anything about but the pride of life, boasting in what has been acquired of this world's good, requires company. These matters are very subtle, and searching, especially when it is remembered that this is addressed to young men with spiritual vigour, in whom the word of God is abiding and who have overcome the evil one. Indeed, it should make us tremble.

John writes not so that we may look at other Christians but at our own hearts. There is this serious tendency to look at others when we are reading the word of God but first of all the scriptures are written in order that we might look at our own hearts. None is immune from these things: 'Wherefore let him that thinketh he standeth take heed lest he fall', 1 Cor. 10. 12.

2. 17 And the world passeth away, and the lust thereof: but he that doeth the will of God abideth for ever.

There is now a contrast between the things of the world and the believer. On the one hand is the transience of the world and, on the other, the permanence of the believer. John speaks of the world with its wrong desires; it is in the process of passing away and will come to nothing. By way of contrast, 'he that doeth the will of God', the child of God whose bent in life is to do the will of God, 'abideth for ever'.

'He that doeth the will of God' refers to Christians. The present continuous speaks of character; if a person belongs to Christ at all, if he is in the family, then this must be the bent of his life. He might fail and lapse, but, characteristically, it is true of him that he desires to do the will of God. In fact, the Lord Jesus, in Matthew chapter 12 verses 49 and 50, indicates that doing the will of the Father is an evidence of a spiritual relationship.

In Romans chapter 12 verse 2 what Paul speaks of is not so much the doing of His will but the proving of it. We prove that good and acceptable and perfect will of God. It is good for us; it is well pleasing to God; it is perfect in its end result. We might not be able to understand it at the time but the end result is perfect.

2. 18 Little children, it is the last time: and as ye have heard that antichrist shall come, even now are there many antichrists; whereby we know that it is the last time.

John has many more things to say to the infants, which are found in verses 18 to 27. In these additions John gives a warning as to antichrists, because infants, in a special way, are exposed to their wiles. In verse 26, he says, 'These things have I written unto you concerning them that seduce you', those who 'lead you astray'.

The word '**time**' is 'hour'. There are different hours. For instance, when the Saviour said, 'mine hour is not yet come', John 2. 4, He was referring to the hour of His suffering on the cross. Here, it is the last hour; the last hour of God's dealings with men as such. There are different expressions regarding time. 1 Timothy chapter 4 verse 1 speaks of 'the latter times'; 'the last days' are mentioned in 2 Timothy chapter 3 verse 1 and 2 Peter chapter 3 verse 3. The 'last days' are spoken of in a different sense in Hebrews chapter 1 verse 2, where the reference is to the last days of God's dealings with the Jews in Old Testament times. The last days in 2 Timothy chapter 3 and 2 Peter chapter 3 are the last days of God's dealings with Gentiles. John is now thinking of the last hour of God's dealing with Gentiles.

There is no definite article before 'hour' because John is not so much referring to a definite time as to a characteristic state. The characteristic state of the last hour was already existing in John's time and was evident; he says, '**even now are there many antichrists**'. However, its fullness will be seen in the last hour of God's dealings with the Gentiles. It is the same in 2 Timothy chapter 3, where Paul speaks of the fact that, 'in last days perilous times shall come'. Even in Timothy's time there were characteristics of the last days, without it actually being the last days. Paul says in 2 Thessalonians chapter 2, 'the mystery of iniquity doth already work'. The manifestation of the lawless one belongs to the last hour but the mystery works now. The manifestation of the antichrist belongs to the last hour but the spirit of antichrist, of antichrists in plurality, existed even in John's day and in ours.

Antichrists involves forerunners of what will be evidenced in the antichrist when he himself is manifested.

John is the only one who speaks of antichrist.[3] 'Anti' has the thought of 'against' but in the sense of 'taking the place of'. It is one who opposes by taking the place of Christ. Even now there are many antichrists, who are forerunners of the antichrist who is yet to appear. John adds, **'whereby we know that it is the last hour'**. In Matthew chapter 24 verse 5, it is not antichrists but false Christs, those who are pretenders to the Messianic office.

2. 19 **They went out from us, but they were not of us; for if they had been of us, they would no doubt have continued with us: but they went out, that they might be made manifest that they were not all of us.**

They went out from us, but they were not of us. John makes it clear that those who went out from them were not of them; they were, in fact, apostates and were antichrist. They had taken up the place of Christian profession but were antichrist in their character. When John says 'they were not of us', he is simply saying that they had a different origin from us altogether.

If they were **'of us they would have continued with us'**. John is teaching here that all who went out were not of them. The statement should read, **'but that they might be manifest that none are of us'**; none who went out were of the family of God. John is not saying here that the child of God never fails but that only those who are not of us, only those who do not belong to the family of God, apostatize. The child of God might fail but it is impossible for such ever to be guilty of apostasy.

This is not primarily ecclesiastical but they would undoubtedly have gone out from the company of Christians where they were. However, that is not what is emphasized; their going out indicated that they were

---

[3] See 2. 18, 22; 4. 3; 2 John 7.

not of God's family but were apostate. In the government of God, it would become clear by their action that they were not of His children. In Jude, apostates crept in unawares, but here they go out from them and the reason is that they were not of the same origin; if they had been they would have continued, not just among them but with them.

This is not the same as in 1 Corinthians chapter 11 verse 19, 'For there must be also heresies among you, that they which are approved may be made manifest among you'. The word 'heresies' has the idea of factions, and those who cause factions are not necessarily apostate. In 'that they which are approved may be made manifest', the approved are those who would avoid factions amongst the people of God. The factions at Corinth were within the assembly and those who were creating them remained in it. The divisions there were at Corinth were still internal but this was the beginning of what would issue in external divisions.

In Acts chapter 5 verse 13, after Ananias and Sapphira were carried out dead, fear fell upon all the church 'and of the rest durst no man join himself to them'. Because of that divine action, in government, there was not only fear in the church but unbelievers would not dare to associate with such a company. However, even as early as Acts chapter 8 a man who makes an empty profession follows Philip the Evangelist, and in Acts chapter 20 Paul says to the Ephesian elders that even from among themselves there shall arise men leading disciples after them.

I take it that the making **manifest** has to do with the government of God in connection with them. It was manifested that they were not of us.

2. 20   But ye have an unction from the Holy One, and ye know all things.

The word '**unction**' is 'anointing'. There is an evident contrast between verses 18 and 20. In verse 18, John speaks of the antichrist, which is simply the anti-anointed one; and he speaks in the same verse of antichrists, anti-anointed ones. By way of contrast, in verse 20, he speaks about the anointed ones; 'ye have an anointing from the holy one'.

'Unction' occurs both here and in verse 27. In the Old Testament, kings, priests and prophets were anointed. The prophet and the king were anointed with oil and the priest was anointed with the holy anointing oil. In each instance, the oil speaks of the Holy Spirit. The anointing here is the anointing of the Holy Spirit and speaks of the gift of the Spirit in grace and power from the Holy One, who is Christ.

The Holy Spirit is spoken of elsewhere in connection with anointing. In Luke chapter 4 verse 18, the Lord says, 'The Spirit of the Lord is upon me, because he hath anointed me to preach the gospel to the poor'. Also, in Acts chapter 10 verse 38, Peter says to Cornelius that 'God anointed Jesus of Nazareth with the Holy Ghost and with power'. In 2 Corinthians chapter 1 verses 20 and 21, Paul says that we have received this anointing; 'Now he which stablisheth us with you in Christ, and hath anointed us, is God; who hath also sealed us, and given the earnest of the Spirit in our hearts'.

The anointing is from **the Holy One**, who is Christ, who is repeatedly spoken of in the scriptures in this way. Psalm 16 verse 10 says, 'For thou wilt not leave my soul in hell; neither wilt thou suffer thine Holy One to see corruption'. In Mark chapter 1 verse 24, the demon said, 'I know thee who thou art, the Holy One of God'. In John chapter 6 verse 69, the King James Version says, in the words of Peter, 'And we believe and are sure that thou art that Christ, the Son of the living God'. This is alternatively rendered, 'We believe and are sure that thou art the holy one of God'. Peter makes the charge in Acts chapter 3 verse 14, that 'ye denied the Holy One and the Just, and desired a murderer to be granted unto you'.

The result of this anointing was that '**ye know all things**'. The Revised Version margin says, 'and ye know all this' but I take it that it should be as we have it here, 'and ye know all things'. '**Ye**' is every child of God, bearing in mind that this is not written to the fathers or to the young men but to the infants. The idea is that they potentially knew all things with conscious, intuitive knowledge. The '**all things**' to which John refers are all things that are necessary relative to the spirit of antichrist that was abroad. It is also true that every child of God, anointed by the

Holy One, has the potential to know all things. When presented with error, perhaps we could not turn to the scriptures and prove it but because we have the Spirit of God within us we intuitively know that it is not the truth. This is true even of the infants.

In John chapter 14 verse 26, the Lord Jesus said that the Holy Spirit would bring to the memory of the apostles what they had heard Him say. Here, however, it is something wider than that which is purely apostolic, belonging even to the infants in God's family. We are, perhaps, not sufficiently aware of what we have as children of God, an anointing from Christ the Holy One, with the potential to know all things. Every one of us has the capacity to know things that the natural man could never understand and be able to aspire to the heights of spiritual truth.

2. 21 I have not written unto you because ye know not the truth, but because ye know it, and that no lie is of the truth.

'**Ye know**' the truth is a remarkable statement because it is made to the infants in God's family. To know the truth is possible only because of what John has said in verse 20. Everyone in God's family, even the infants, have the anointing of the Holy Spirit that they receive from Christ the Holy One.

What John says here was to guard them against those who would offer what was a pretence of fresh light or new doctrine, introduced by the antichrists. John indicates that he was not writing to them because they did not know the truth but because they knew it. Therefore, they did not need to be swayed or influenced by what was presented as new light or new doctrine.

John adds, '**no lie is of the truth**'. If there is contained in any purported fresh light or new doctrine anything that is not of the truth and is a lie, then it is not of the truth. We need to remember this today, when we are surrounded by so many evil cults, that one lie is all that is required to expose their teaching as being not of the truth.

2. 22 Who is a liar but he that denieth that Jesus is the Christ? He is antichrist, that denieth the Father and the Son.

The definite article is employed here; '**who is a liar**' is really 'who is the liar'. John is not speaking of 'the liar' in an absolute sense but argumentatively. He is not thinking of the devil. In verse 21, he says that 'no lie is of the truth', presenting truth in the abstract, but now he presents it in the concrete, 'who then is the liar'. If no lie is of the truth, the liar is **he that denieth that Jesus is the Christ**, denying His Messiahship. Once they took their place as being Christians, but, in fact, they belong to the lie.

There is no article before 'antichrist' in verse 18 but there is here. '**He is antichrist**' is, 'He is the antichrist'. Again, John is just employing an argument; the antichrist is this man. Just as the liar of this verse is not Satan, so here the antichrist is not necessarily the beast in Revelation chapter 13. Thus, it is 'the antichrist', embracing here both Jews and Gentiles who had once professed Christianity.

To deny that Jesus is the Christ particularly has in mind a Jew who may have professed the Christian faith but who now makes this denial. To deny **the Father and the Son** has more in mind a Gentile who once professed the Christian faith but now denies the Father and the Son. That the Father and the Son should alike be honoured, (see John chapter 5 verse 23) is brought out in the next verse.

It seems that these antichrists imbibed new light and new doctrine. They were against Christ by setting themselves up as a new kind of Christian, believing in a new kind of Christ other than He who is brought before us in the New Testament.

2. 23 Whosoever denieth the Son, the same hath not the Father: (but) he that acknowledgeth the Son hath the Father also.

Whilst the King James Version italicises the last part of the verse most other translations appear to accept its genuineness. This makes this verse to be very interesting. In the first part of the verse we have a denial with a warning, whilst the second part contains a confession with encouragement.

John is speaking of a denial or a confession of **the Son**. Whether a person denies the Son or confesses Him is always the acid test of reality. Any who deny the Son have not the Father. Unitarians, including Jehovah's Witnesses, deny the Son and so they cannot have God as Father. To confess the Son, however, is to have the Son and to have the Father also. To confess the Father, as Unitarians and Jehovah's Witnesses do, but to deny the Son, is worthless. A man stands or falls on his attitude to the Son. The test is, 'What think ye of Christ?' Matt. 22. 42.

We cannot honour God more than by honouring His Son; there is none so precious to God as He is. That is why He says, 'For the Father himself loveth you, because ye have loved me, and have believed that I came out from God', John 16. 27.

He was never other than the Son of God, from eternity to eternity. There are many scriptures that would indicate the error of saying that He became the Son at incarnation. If there was a time when God was not the Father then there was a time when the Lord Jesus was not the Son. A man does not become a father until he has a son but the analogy fails in relation to the Godhead. The fact that Christ is Son does not mean that the Father is antecedent to Him; if there was a time when He was not the Son then there was a time when God was not the Father.

2. 24 **Let that therefore abide in you which ye have heard from the beginning. If that which ye have heard from the beginning shall remain in you, ye also shall continue in the Son, and in the Father.**

The Revised Version says here, **'as for you let that abide in you'**. It signifies 'as for you' in contrast to those antichrists, those liars.

The expression '**from the beginning**' must always be understood in its context. They had heard from the beginning of the apostles' testimony to them the truth with regard to the Son of God. There can be no improvement on this, and so 'Let that therefore abide in you', or 'remain in you', means that they were not to admit anything new or permit anything in addition to the revelation of God to them, through the apostles, concerning the Son. They were to let what they had been taught from the beginning have a home in their heart.

A plurality of persons in the Godhead is clearly taught in many places in the Old Testament. For instance, 'Let us make man in our image', Gen. 1. 26, involves plurality of persons. However, the revelation of the Father, the Son, and the Holy Spirit belongs particularly to this present era. The Israelites knew God as Jehovah and as Elohim, both names involving a plurality of persons in the Godhead. The Jews knew, of course, that a son was not one whit inferior to his father. They accused Jesus of blasphemy because He 'said also that God was his Father, making himself equal with God', John 5. 18.

'**Ye also shall continue in the Son, and in the Father**'. If the truth regarding the Son and the Father had a home in their heart, they would, in turn, find a home in the heart of the Son and in the heart of the Father.

2. 25 And this is the promise that he hath promised us, even eternal life.

John quite frequently uses the expression 'this is'. In chapter 3 verse 23, 'this is his commandment'. In chapter 5 verse 11, 'this is the record'. Here it is, '**this is the promise**'. This has a connection with verse 24, in which John speaks of abiding in the Father and the Son. This leads John to think of eternal life, 'And this is life eternal, that they might know thee the only true God, and Jesus Christ, whom thou hast sent', John 17. 3. This is the promise that the Lord promised the apostles when He was here. He said, for instance in John chapter 4 verse 14, 'the water that I shall give him shall be in him a well of water springing up into everlasting life'. Again, 'And this is the will of him that sent me, that every one which seeth the Son, and believeth on him, may have everlasting life', John 6. 40.

Paul speaks of 'the hope of eternal life, which God, that cannot lie, promised before the world began', Titus 1. 2. There, the promise was given to mankind before the world began, but here it is the promise that He has promised 'us', the apostles. It is Christ, therefore, who is particularly in view here as the one who gave the promise.

2. 26   These things have I written unto you concerning them that seduce you.

John now wants to warn them that though they knew the truth there were those who would **seduce** them, who would lead them astray. John is referring again to the warnings that he has already given concerning the antichrists.

John tells us two things about them. In verse 19, 'they went out, that they might be made manifest that they were not all of us'. In verse 22, they are characterized by the lie in respect of the person of Christ. As we have seen, it is evident from verse 22 that John has in mind not only the Jew but the professing Christian.

2. 27   But the anointing which ye have received of him abideth in you, and ye need not that any man teach you: but as the same anointing teacheth you of all things, and is truth, and is no lie, and even as it hath taught you, ye shall abide in him.

In this verse John, as his custom was, uses repetition for the purpose of emphasis. In verse 20, he says, 'ye know all things'; now he says, 'teacheth you concerning all things'. In verse 21, he says, 'no lie is of the truth'; now he says, 'is truth and no lie'. In verse 24, he says, 'ye shall abide in the Son'; now he says, 'ye shall abide in him'.

'The anointing which ye have received of him abideth in you,' is a note of confidence based on fact. This anointing is received on believing, as we have already seen, but now John adds that what we have received abides with us. The Spirit of God is never withdrawn. In verse 24, the truth they had heard abode in them; here, the anointing abode in them. The anointing is that by which they would enjoy the truth in respect of the Son and the Father.

They did not need any man to teach them because, in verse 20, he had said, 'ye know all things'. This does not mean that we do not need divinely given teachers among God's people, for the Lord has given them, Eph. 4. 11. What the apostle is saying is that the children of God did not need to heed, to run after or to fear these seducers. It is from the standpoint that they did not need to hear what these men said that John is speaking when he says, '**ye need not that any man teach you**'. 'Ye know all things' is not in an unqualified sense. To know all things is to be omniscient. Each one of us has different capacities, and we know according to our divinely given capacity; but what John is saying here is that we each have an anointing from the Holy One and we know all things potentially, with regard to the truth of the Father and the Son which was being denied.

'**Teacheth you of all things**' is 'teacheth you about all things'. The Spirit, His anointing, teaches you. Again, the tense here is the present continuous; His anointing teaches you continuously and progressively and is truth. The Spirit is the Spirit of truth and is no lie; the Spirit of truth can never admit of any falsehood that the seducers were, no doubt, suggesting to them.

We know all things potentially, not because of the Spirit of God personally as a gift of grace but because of the Spirit of God as an anointing. The Spirit of God as an anointing is not just the gift of the person of the Spirit but the anointing is the power of the Spirit operating in heart and life. If we are not giving the Spirit of God His rightful place and are not allowing Him to operate in power through the word on our hearts and minds, then we are open to error. It all depends on what we are feeding, and the level of my communion. If we are out of touch with God, the Spirit is grieved and we do not enjoy His presence and power as an anointing. It is, therefore, a matter of being right with

God so that the ungrieved Spirit, as the anointing, can move in power in our hearts. It is one thing to have the Spirit personally but it is another thing to be in that condition in which the Spirit of God can, as the Spirit of truth, teach us all things, as He would desire.

When John is dealing with the deceivers in chapter 4, he tells us to put the deceivers to the test in a twofold way, relating to the word of God and the Son of God. The tests are whether their teaching agrees or conflicts with the word of God on the one hand, and the truth of the Son of God on the other.

Three manifestations, 2. 28 – 3. 15

1. A future manifestation.
    Associated with His servants, v. 28
    Associated with His saints, or His children, v. 2

2. A past manifestation.
    Connected with sins, v. 5
    Connected with Satan, v. 8

3. A present manifestation.
    Of the children of God, v. 10
    Of the children of the devil, v. 10

2. 28 **And now, little children, abide in him; that, when he shall appear, we may have confidence, and not be ashamed before him at his coming.**

Firstly, John treats of the future manifestation as it relates to the servants, vv. 28, 29. John is appealing to the family of God on the basis of the apostles' deep interest in them. The apostles, those who served their interests, and ministered to them the truth of God, want to see them with a full reward in that day. In that case, the apostles shall not be ashamed before Him at His coming.

Here, John resumes the teaching of verses 1 to 11 and, once again, refers to all the children in God's family as he addresses them as '**dear children**'. He is addressing the whole family of God as it pertains to the entire dispensation, but he is thinking particularly of those who came under the sound of the ministry of the apostles, even though at the time he wrote most of these had died. They had heard them from the beginning.

'**Abide in him**', that is Christ. This is a command rather than an exhortation. Abiding in Him ought to be the normal experience and condition of every child of God. It is different to being in Him. Also, it is not just recognizing that one needs Christ and could not live without Him; this is, relatively, low ground and all who are saved might feel this way. Rather, it means that having learned to distrust self altogether the child of God is cleaving to Him. His heart has become completely captivated with the incomparable worth of His person and He means everything to him. John has in mind that where this was so the reward would be given that the apostles would love to see them having.

A child of God can put himself in the position where he is not abiding in Christ, not dwelling in Him, not finding his home in Him. This will be the case if there is any unjudged sin in the life and if other things are satisfying the heart, or even have a place there, displacing Christ in my affections. This is very high ground; but Christianity is, of course, very high ground. We do well to ask ourselves whether there is anything in our lives that would hinder us abiding in Him in an experiential way.

'**That when he shall appear**'. This should be rendered, 'if he be manifested'. This is not an 'if' of doubt as to the fact of it, nor is it an 'if' of doubt as to the time of it; it is an 'if' of argument only. It is connected with the thought 'that we may have confidence'. They were to abide in Christ, that 'if he appears, **we may have confidence**'. 'Confidence' or 'boldness' means 'freedom of speaking' or 'frankness'.

'**And not be ashamed**' means not shrinking with shame before Him '**at his coming**'. John uses the word *parousia* in speaking of His coming. The word relates not just to the act of His coming but to the fact of His presence. Here, it relates to His presence in relation to His appearing rather than His presence in relation to the rapture. The apostles would be ashamed if those dear children did not abide in Him; then, the apostles would have a sense of shame that there was so little or no reward for those amongst whom they had laboured.

We are suffering today from too many professional preachers who think that all that is involved in preaching is giving an intellectually correct address but who do not have the present interests and eternal well-being of the saints in their heart. We ought to stop being like this and be more like the apostles in this regard.

2. 29   If ye know that he is righteous, ye know that every one that doeth righteousness is born of him.

The words translated '**know**' are different. 'If ye know', intuitively, 'that he is righteous, ye know', or recognize with inward, conscious knowledge 'that everyone that doeth righteousness is born of him'.

John is speaking here of one of the evidences of the new birth; '**every one who doeth righteousness is born of God**'. In John's writings care has to be taken to sort out exactly to whom he is referring when he uses the pronoun 'he'. In writing as he does, John leaves us in no doubt as to the equality of the Son with the Father. 'If ye know that **he** is righteous' refers to Christ but 'ye know that everyone that doeth righteousness is born of **him**' refers to being born of God. It might be argued that in chapter 1 verse 9 it is God who is righteous, just as in chapter 2 verse 1 Jesus is righteous, for He is 'Jesus Christ the righteous one'. Therefore, John speaks in this Epistle of both the Father and the Son as being righteous. It might also be argued that 'born of him' does not exclude the possibility that it means 'born of Christ', for the Son 'quickeneth whom he will', John 5. 21. There could be arguments either way but I believe that John is stating that Christ is righteous, as are all those who are born of God. The new nature, communicated to the children of God on the occasion of the new birth, is divine and John deduces the important truth that if He is righteous then those who partake of this new nature must practice righteousness.

'Doeth righteousness' is a word that occurs frequently in John's Epistle. It speaks of an action that is continued or not yet complete; what one does continually or repeatedly. The significance of the present continuous tense is that it speaks of character; the character of those who have been born of Him is that they practise righteousness. The bent of their life is to do what is right. This, of course, is not sinless perfection, of which the Bible says nothing. The child of God might fail but his bent is to do righteousness. An unregenerate man can act righteously on occasions but to do so is not the character, or bent, of his life. 'There is none righteousness, no, not one', Rom. 3. 10.

This is the first occurrence of the expression **'born of him'** in this Epistle. Other occurrences are found in chapter 3 verse 9, 'whosoever is born of God doth not commit sin; for his seed remaineth in him; and he cannot sin, because he is born of God'; in chapter 4 verse 7, 'everyone that loveth is born of God, and knoweth God'; and in chapter 5 verse 1, 'whosoever believeth that Jesus is the Christ is born of God'. The new birth is entirely of God.

Chapter 3

3. 1 Behold, what manner of love the Father hath bestowed upon us, that we should be called the sons of God: therefore the world knoweth us not, because it knew him not.

The delightful connection between the closing verse of chapter 2 and the opening verse of chapter 3 must be observed. John moves from the practice of righteousness, in chapter 2 verse 29, to the enjoyment of love. He also moves from the thought of being born of God to speaking of the children of God. Again, John is speaking in chapter 2 verse 29 of how we know those who are born of God, but here he is saying that the world does not know the children of God. Further, in chapter 2 verse 29, John says that we know those who are born of God because we know Him, but here the world does not know the children of God because it knows Him not.

'Behold' is simply 'see'; 'see **what manner of love**'. John is not here speaking of the measure of divine love so much as he is speaking of the wonder of it. Some have suggested that the thought is that it is something from outside of this realm in which we live. In Luke chapter 1 verse 29, Mary contemplates 'what manner of salutation' she received from Gabriel. It was a salutation from another country, from another realm. Similarly, in Mark chapter 4 verse 41, the question is asked, 'What manner of man is this?' He was from another realm. The wonder of divine love is that despite what we were we are now divinely called the children of God.

This love is not just shown but it is **bestowed**, given, imparted for children to enjoy; and the purpose of His love is **that we might be called**, by the Father, the children of God.

'Sons of God' should read 'children of God'. **Therefore**, for this cause, alluding to what has preceded, **the world knoweth us not**. We are an enigma to the world as the children of God. **It knew Him not**, in that it failed to recognize or understand God's Son as such; and it knows us not as being those who have relationship to God, a nature from God, and the enjoyment of the love of the Father. The world cannot understand these things. We have been brought to share things that this world knows nothing about and if the world knows us not then we share with Christ what He experienced when He was here, for it knew Him not.

The difference between children and sons is a marked one. In John's writings, he speaks of God's people as the children of God, save for one occasion, in Revelation chapter 21 verse 7, where he speaks of them as the 'sons' of God. The verse says, 'He that overcometh shall inherit all things; and I will be his God, and he shall be my son'. It is, in fact, a quotation from Zechariah chapter 8. Paul speaks of us as sons, whereas John speaks of us as children. Paul takes up the legal side, under the Roman law, where adoption was equivalent to parentage, but John speaks of the children of God, in terms of generation. 'Children' just means 'born ones', and all who are born of God are the children of God. It involves the birthday. Sonship involves something more, speaking of dignity and position. There is no such thing as some of God's people being children and not being sons, for in Galatians chapter 3 verse 26 we are all the sons of God by faith in Christ Jesus. However, while we are sons of God by faith we might not be necessarily sons of God in character. To be sons of God characteristically we must be led by the Spirit of God, Rom. 8. 14. This involves dispossessing ourselves of everything that hinders the Spirit of God being in complete control in our lives. That makes me to be characteristically what I am by faith. There is also another thought, that we are now the children of God but sonship in its fullest sense belongs to the future. This involves both moral and physical conformity to Christ. He is bringing many sons to glory, and sonship in its fullness will not be realized until those of us who are children have been 'conformed to the image of his Son', Rom. 8. 29.

3. 2 **Beloved, now are we the sons of God, and it doth not yet appear what we shall be: but we know that, when he shall appear, we shall be like him; for we shall see him as he is.**

In this verse there is the second aspect of the future manifestation. The connection seems to be that in verse 1 it is children but in verse 2 it is sonship. Sonship in its fullest sense is just to be like Him.

'Beloved' occurs in chapter 2 verse 7; chapter 3 verses 2 and 21; chapter 4 verses 1, 7 and 11. The great theme of love now becomes the main theme in this Epistle, the word 'love' occurring sixteen times. As a verb it occurs twenty-five times and as an adjective five times.

The word '**now**' has a delightful significance when seen in conjunction with the expressions '**not yet**' and '**we shall be**'. These are, of course, time terms. John assures us that we are now the children of God. The wonder of this should fill our hearts; we know assuredly that we are now the children of God. However, that is not the end of it for when He shall appear we shall be like Him. Some render '**when he shall appear**', or be manifested, as 'when it is manifested'. If it is 'it shall be manifested' then it relates to what we shall be but if it is 'he shall be manifested' the reference is to God's Son, and I believe that this is the case. Again, the word 'if' does not introduce doubt; it is an 'if' of argument. We must remember that we are not just going to be like Him when He appears in glory but we shall be like Him at the rapture; at His coming to the air and not at His manifestation. Therefore, some render the expression, 'If He shall be manifested, we shall be like Him', because we shall have already met Him in the air and been with Him for some time.

The sequence of thought here is, first of all, Christ must now be hidden, if He is going to be manifested. In Acts chapter 1 verse 9, a cloud received Him 'out of their sight'. In Hebrews chapter 6 verse 19, He has entered 'into that within the veil'. In Colossians chapter 3 verse 3, the apostle says, 'your life is hid with Christ in God' but goes on to say, 'When Christ, who is our life, shall appear'. The one in whom we trust is hidden and it is because of Him that we are born of God. A day is soon coming, however, when the one who is now hidden shall be manifested and we are going to be manifested with Him. We shall share His glory, the stigma shall be rolled away, the world's lack of understanding shall disappear and its reproach shall be done for ever.

Moral likeness to Christ is connected with the present in chapter 2 verse 29, but the rapture and His appearing are rather connected with physical likeness to Him. **'We shall be like him'**, conformed to His image. This will not involve things that are true only of deity, such as omniscience, but we shall think as He thinks and see as He sees.

We are so unlike him now, in every way, but we shall be like Him then. God has no higher thought than His own Son, and God, who has upon His heart our highest good, is going to make us like Him. **We shall see Him**, not as He was on the cross, when His visage was marred more than any man and His form more than the sons of men, nor as He will be, when He sits on the great white throne, when from before His face the earth and the heaven flee away; but **as He is** now, at God's right hand, with all the favour, pleasure and acceptance of God resting upon Him. When we are manifested with Him in glory, it is not the glory of His Father's house but the glory of His kingdom. The world will see that, but we alone shall see Him as He is; that is private and belongs to the Father's house. What a debt of love we owe Him, such that we can never repay.

3. 3 And every man that hath this hope in him purifieth himself, even as he is pure.

This is the moral effect of this hope. **Every man** means, simply, 'everyone', an expression frequently used by John; here he speaks of everyone who has this great **hope**. It is not the thought of hope within the believer as an individual but hope set on Christ, the hope of being like Him. Paul uses a similar expression, 'on him', in Romans chapter 15 verse 12, when he says, 'On him shall the Gentiles trust'.

The moral effect of this hope is that the one who has it purifies himself, even as **He is pure**. This is an absolute statement, regarding a purity that cannot be tarnished. It is the same in verse 5, where John says, 'in him is no sin'. In the New Testament, as well as the Old Testament, the verb 'purify' is used of external, ceremonial cleansing; see, for instance, John chapter 11 verse 55 and Acts chapter 21 verse 24. However, it is also used of inward purification (see, for instance, 1 Peter chapter 1 verse 22) and this is the thought here.

This purifying is not something that God does for me but it is something I do for myself. It involves personal effort and exercise. On the Day of Atonement, when the priest would enter into the holiest, he first of all had to visit the laver. However, we are not just going into the sanctuary; we are going to see Him, who is pure and uncontaminated, and we are going to be like Him. Having this hope set on Him we purify ourselves, keeping ourselves free from this world's contaminations.

3. 4 Whosoever committeth sin transgresseth also the law: for sin is the transgression of the law

Having considered His future manifestation, John now considers the past manifestation of the Son of God. This is twofold, connected with sins, v. 5, and Satan, v. 8.

There is no thought in this verse of the **law** of Moses. The statement in this verse applies equally to the Jew, who was under the law, and to the Gentile, who was not under the law and possibly knew nothing about it. The verse should read, 'Everyone that doeth sin doeth also lawlessness; and sin is lawlessness'. The word does not mean, 'the transgression of the law' but, rather, 'lawlessness'. In the expression 'everyone that doeth sin' the reference is not simply to a person 'committing a sin' but, rather, 'doing sin'; it is a reference to the practice of sin. **Lawlessness** simply means self-will, expressed in independence of God, having no regard for Him, being insubordinate to Him. It is not specifically acting against the law.

During the period referred to by Paul in Romans chapter 5, when the law had not yet been given, sin reigned because men were lawless. It was not just that they were without the law, though that is true, but they were acting in self-will and in independence of God. It is the same word that is translated 'iniquity' in Titus chapter 2 verse 14. In our unconverted days, we were characterized by self-will and living in independence of God, but the death of Christ has delivered us from that. If we still live such a life then we might question whether we have been born of God at all. Self-will should never enter into the Christian life, for it is not characteristic of Christianity.

3. 5   And ye know that he was manifested to take away our sins; and in him is no sin.

The thought of Christ's manifestation, at His incarnation, is dealt with fairly extensively in the New Testament. Paul tells us **how He was manifested**; 'great is the mystery of godliness; God was manifest in the flesh', 1 Tim. 3. 16. He was manifested in this world in the flesh, taking part in flesh and blood, Heb. 2. 14, and in the likeness of sinful flesh, Rom. 8. 3. John, however, tells us **why He was manifested** and gives two reasons. 'He was manifested to take away our sins', v. 5, and that He 'might destroy the works of the devil', v. 8. John tells us **He was manifested**, therefore, to deal with sins and to deal with the devil. The Apostle Peter tells us **when He was manifested**; Christ 'was manifested in these last times for you', 1 Pet. 1. 20. 'These last times' indicate that He was manifested 'at the end of those times', when God had made abundantly clear the total inadequacy of every other sacrifice to take away sins. Peter also tells us **for whom He was manifested** when in the same verse he says it was 'for you' and this ought to strike a chord in our hearts.

The purpose of His manifestation was to **take away our sins**. John does not tell us here how he would take away sins but rather just deals with the purpose of His manifestation. If we want to know how He did it we would have to turn to other scriptures, such as Hebrews chapter 9 verse 26, 'he appeared to put away sin by the sacrifice of himself', or 1 Peter chapter 2 verse 24, 'who his own self bare our sins in his own body on the tree'.

John is not speaking of His work but of the wonder of His person. John's thought is that sin is so abhorrent to God that He went to such lengths to have sins taken away; it cost Him nothing less than the one in whom is no sin. John, as is his wont, is emphasizing the abhorrence of sin to God.

The phrase '**and in him is no sin**' is often misquoted as, 'in him was no sin'. There is a big difference. When John says, 'in him is no sin' he makes a statement that is absolute, indicating that there neither was, nor could there ever be, sin in Him. In 1 Peter chapter 2 verse 22, Peter says, He 'did no sin'. Peter is not there referring to the impeccability of Christ, because His impeccability consists not in the fact that He did not sin but in that He could not sin. The reason why He could not sin is that in Him is no sin at all; the statement is absolute. In 1 Peter chapter 2 verse 22, the word for 'sin' is 'fault'. Peter tells Christian domestic servants that if they were buffeted for well doing they were to think of the one who never did any fault. He was buffeted but, in these specific circumstances, He never sinned.

Notice that the truth of verse 5 is sandwiched between two very important pronouncements. In verse 4, John tells us what sin is; it is the transgression of the law. In verse 6, John tells us that sinning is incompatible with knowing Christ.

3. 6 Whosoever abideth in him sinneth not: whosoever sinneth hath not seen him, neither known him.

The statements here are antithetical. Abiding in Christ is normal Christian life and experience. It is looking to Christ, cleaving to Him and delighting in Him. '**Whosoever abideth in Him sinneth not**'. 'Sinneth' is in the present continuous tense; once again, John is speaking of character. He does not say, 'whosoever abideth in him never sins' but 'whosoever abideth in him sinneth not'. This is not the character of the one who abides in Christ; it is not the bent of his life. John is saying that the person who abides in Him does not habitually sin. One may lapse into sin, as the opening verses of chapter 2 teach, but this is not the bent of life. The secret of not sinning is not a negative approach to things, or the fear of retribution; it is to continually abide in Him. This is something even greater than an acknowledgement of divine holiness. Abiding in Him is where Christ's incomparable worth has completely won my heart, meaning more to me than anything else. 'Whosoever abideth in him sinneth not'.

'**Whosoever sinneth hath not seen him, neither known him**'. Again, the tense is present continuous and John is speaking, therefore, of everyone whose character is habitually or continually to sin. This is to sin without conscience or thought of confession and without contrition. Such a person has neither seen Him by faith nor known Him as to His character. It is important to observe these present continuous tenses and their significance or John's Epistle will never be rightly understood.

3. 7   Little children, let no man deceive you: he that doeth righteousness is righteous, even as he is righteous.

This leads John on, in the next verse, to speak of the Son of God destroying the works of the devil. The devil's work from the beginning has been in relation to this matter of deception and so John will there speak of the Son of God being manifested that He might destroy, or undo, or unloose the works of the devil.

John is saying that no matter what people might say, or how they may try to lead you astray from this, anyone who does righteousness is '**righteous, even as he is righteous**'. It is a test of a man being born of God; 'by their fruits ye shall know them', Matt. 7. 20.

The practice of righteousness must have its source in the one who is Himself righteous. Of course, to be philanthropic is a right thing but the source of, or motive for, the act might be wrong. In Romans chapter 3 verse 10, we are told that 'there is none righteous'; an unregenerate man does not habitually and continuously practise righteous acts. In tracing things to their source, John draws the contrast between God's Son and the devil. In verse 7, it is God's Son, whereas in verse 8 it is the devil.

3. 8   He that committeth sin is of the devil; for the devil sinneth from the beginning. For this purpose the Son of God was manifested, that he might destroy the works of the devil.

In chapter 2 verse 29, John has already said that 'everyone that doeth righteousness is born of him'. Then, in chapter 3 verse 7, he says, 'he that doeth righteousness is righteous' (that is, his nature is righteous), 'even as he is righteous' (that is, Christ is righteous as to His nature). Now, John says, 'he that committeth sin' (the word is, he that 'doeth' sin) 'is of the devil'. The habitual practice of righteousness and sin are thus contrasted in verses 7 and 8. The person who 'doeth sin' has this as his character, his habit; and he has no sense of guilt and no thought of confession.

Such a person is, as to his character, of the devil, for the devil habitually **sinneth from the beginning**. The devil does not cease to sin; 'sinneth' is, again, in the present continuous tense. This is his character from the beginning of his being the devil. Thus, if anyone sins habitually and continuously, he is in the character of the one who sinneth from the beginning.

The **works of the devil** and the devil sinning **from the beginning** involve, in the first instance, pride in the devil's heart as he endeavoured to usurp God's place. The devil undoubtedly felt that God was holding back something from him. Secondly, with regard to man, the devil sinned by misrepresenting God, in that he said to our first parents that God was keeping something back from them and so deceived them. The particular sin of the devil, therefore, is to misrepresent God by portraying Him as a withholder or an exactor making unreasonable demands. However, the manifestation of God's Son has destroyed forever such a deception because God having given His own dear Son it could never again be argued that God is like this.

Death is the result of man's own sin rather than being one of the works of the devil, 'by one man sin entered into the world, and death by sin', Rom. 5. 12. The devil is the one who had authority over death, Heb. 2. 14, rather than it being one of his works.

3. 9   **Whosoever is born of God doth not commit sin; for his seed remaineth in him: and he cannot sin, because he is born of God.**

'**Whosoever is**' or hath been 'born of God doth not commit sin'. The expression '**doth not commit sin**' is really 'doeth not sin' or 'does not practise sin' JND. Here is one of the evidences of having been born of God. Observe, again, the importance of the tenses in this Epistle. Once again it is the present continuous tense that John employs. 'Whosoever is born of God' or hath been born of God 'does not habitually practise sin' and this is because **'his seed remaineth in him'**. The Apostle John is simply referring to divine life communicated by divine quickening. This is quite different to the seed of the word of God, as we have in the parable of the sower. This is rather the seed that is brought before us in 1 Peter chapter 1 verse 23, where Peter speaks of 'Being born again not of corruptible seed, but of incorruptible, by the word of God which liveth and abideth for ever'. This is not the word of God itself but the Spirit of God, through the word, producing an incorruptible seed. Let us observe, once again, that John employs the present continuous tense. His seed, that is this divine life, 'remaineth in him'. There is absolutely no thought anywhere in the New Testament of a fall-away doctrine. Once a person is possessed with this divine life, the seed remains in him and never leaves him.

'And he cannot sin because he is' or 'has been' **'born of God'**. This presents a problem to some who might think that there is a contradiction between this verse and what is stated in chapter 2 verse 1, that 'If any man sin, we have an advocate with the Father'. When John says 'he cannot sin', he is thinking of the believer identified with the seed, with the new nature that is within him; and being identified with it, and not the old nature, he cannot sin. It is not simply that 'he doeth not sin' but that 'he cannot sin'.

In chapter 5 verse 18, John says, 'Whosoever is born of God sinneth not' but this is somewhat different. In that verse 'sinneth not' is 'sinneth not' habitually or characteristically, but here there is a complete negative; he cannot sin under any circumstance. Thus, the reference must be to the believer identified with the divine nature, the seed that abides in him. It is quite a common thing in the word of God for the believer to be identified either with the old nature or the new nature.

3. 10 In this the children of God are manifest, and the children of the devil: whosoever doeth not righteousness is not of God, neither he that loveth not his brother.

John now considers the present manifestation of those who are the children of God and those who are the children of the devil. They are manifest by the life that they live and the works that they perform.

Four things characterize the children of God. They do not commit sin, v. 9; they love each other, v. 11; they are hated of the world, v. 13; and there is a conscious knowledge of salvation, v. 14. Then, in this verse, John speaks of two things that characterize the children of the devil; they do not righteousness and love not their brother.

'**Whosoever**', or 'everyone who' '**doeth not righteousness is not of God**'. In chapter 2 verse 29, John says, 'Ye know that everyone that doeth righteousness is born of him' but here the opposite is stated; if a person is not of God he is unable to keep His commandments. He who loves not his brother abides in death and anyone who abides in death is incapable of keeping His commandments.

3. 11 For this is the message that ye heard from the beginning, that we should love one another.

The expression 'from the beginning' is always to be understood in the light of its context. John is writing to people who had heard an announcement **from the beginning**, which must have been teaching that they heard from the apostles. 'From the beginning' in this verse does not have the same meaning as the same expression in chapter 1 verse 1, where the reference is to the beginning of the Lord's public ministry, because the recipients of John's letter were not with Him to have been able to hear Him. Here, however, the reference is to the beginning of the apostolic ministry that they had heard. The apostles had communicated what they had learnt from the Saviour and it is from this communication they had learned that they should love one another. The message they heard from the beginning, therefore, was not the message of the law, in the matter of loving one's neighbour as oneself, but the message that the apostles had received from Christ, a new commandment. This is associated with the family of God.

John often speaks about having love one to another. Five times in his Gospel and five times in his first Epistle he says, **'love one another'**. He emphasizes this more than the other writers because he always has the thought of God's people as a family as the background to his teaching. It is family love, brotherly love, the love of children. John's thinking is not that we are members of the body or subjects in the kingdom but that we are children in a family. John develops this in chapter 5 verse 1, where he says that if we love Him who begat us then we must love those who are begotten of Him, because we are in the same family, begotten from the same source. Hence, he emphasizes the word 'love'.

In the circle of the family there is love for one another. As far as the world outside is concerned we cannot expect anything but hatred. There is love on the inside and hatred on the outside. That is John's presentation of truth. The Lord Jesus taught us to love our enemies and pray for those who despitefully use us. If we are to love our enemies, how much more intense ought our love to be for those who are our brethren.

3. 12   Not as Cain, who was of that wicked one, and slew his brother. And wherefore slew he him? Because his own works were evil, and his brother's righteous.

Verse 12 is an expansion, by way of illustration, of the teaching of verse 10. In verse 10 the children of the devil are manifest; in verse 12, Cain was of that wicked, or evil, one. In verse 10, 'whosoever doeth not righteousness is not of God' and, in verse 12, Cain's works were evil. In verse 10, it says, 'Neither he that loveth not his brother' and, in verse 12, Cain slew his brother, because his works were evil and his brother's righteous.

Now it is interesting to observe the pattern, the definite design, in John's writing. Notice, in verse 8, he says that 'the devil sinneth from the beginning' of his being such, and in verse 12 he goes back to the first man that was born, Cain. He **slew his brother** because he was of the evil one. Again, in verse 8, he says that 'he that committeth sin is of the devil' and, in verse 10, he speaks of the children of the devil who do not righteousness and love not. Further, in verse 12, Cain was **of that wicked one** and his works were evil. The thought is that he was not just evil in his character and ways, but it was in his mind actually to pursue evil. Cain was of the wicked one in that he was morally like him.

A most important matter is raised in the question, '**And wherefore slew he him?**' Perhaps our immediate answer would be that it was because God had rejected Cain's offering but that is not John's answer. John indicates that Cain's works were evil and his brother's righteous. This was, in fact, before their offerings were brought. It is important to see that the offering of Cain only brought to a head and exposed Cain's evil character.

It is true that his offering was rejected because it was not acceptable but the reason he offered that which was not acceptable was that it was in keeping with the man's life. Abel's offering was a witness that he was righteous; what he offered was the product of his life.

3.13   Marvel not, my brethren, if the world hate you.

Here is yet another feature of those who are the children of God; they are hated of the world. This verse is an expansion of the previous one. In verse 12, John tells us that Cain slew his brother, and now he says, '**Marvel not**', or wonder not, '**my brethren, if the world hate you**'. John is thinking predominantly of Cain's world in its hatred of righteousness; it is no wonder if it hates you.

This is the only occurrence of John addressing those to whom he writes as '**brethren**'. It is in chapter 2 verse 7 in the King James Version but there it should read 'beloved'. He speaks of his brethren here because he has been thinking in terms of brotherly love.

3. 14 We know that we have passed from death unto life, because we love the brethren. He that loveth not his brother abideth in death.

'**We know**' refers to conscious knowledge that the children of God have of salvation, that we have passed out of the sphere of death, where there is hate, into the sphere of life where there is love. We consciously know this because we love the brethren. John teaches that the love of the brethren is a necessary evidence of salvation.

In John chapter 13 verse 35 the Lord Jesus says, 'By this shall all men know that ye are my disciples, if ye have love one to another'. In John's Gospel our love for one another is evidence to the world that we belong to Christ, but in John's Epistle it is rather different; it is an inward witness in ourselves that we have passed from death unto life. There is, then, a twofold evidence to the world and within ourselves arising from the fact that we love one another.

John then continues to deal with the children of the evil one, continuing on from what he has said in the preceding two verses. '**Loveth**' is in the present continuous tense. John is here dealing with character rather than isolated lapses in the life of any individual. There may be lapses, but if there is a persistent absence of love in my heart toward a brother then I might question whether I am born of God at all. Indeed, hatred in oneself is an evidence of being in the sphere of death.

Notice that John does not say that person 'is in death' but that he 'abideth in death'. This is because it is Cain's religious world that he has in view and a man in it who professes something different from what is true. He abideth in death despite his profession. '**Brother**' is here an assumed relationship, because he is moving in that sphere though he is not actually his brother because he still abides in death.

3. 15 Whosoever hateth his brother is a murderer: and ye know that no murderer hath eternal life abiding in him.

'**Hateth**' is again in the present continuous tense. John is going beyond conduct here. Continual hatred in the heart is equal to an act of murder. In principle it is the same. It has been pointed out that a court of law allows a man to hate but not to murder and that you cannot be judged for what you think or how you feel. That is not true of God, who deals with the heart and motives, not just actions. The Lord Jesus said in His sermon on the mount that He came not to destroy the law but rather to fill it out. He did this by His teaching in that sermon. The law dealt with actions but the sermon on the mount deals with motives. He spoke of the act of committing adultery but went on to speak of the heart and the motive when He spoke about the lustful look. Thus, God is not just concerned with actions but takes into account the heart and motives. The motive in hatred is just the same as murder '**and no murder hath eternal life abiding in Him**'. It is impossible that hatred and murder could abide together with eternal life.

A distinction must be made between hating deeds and hating persons. I must hate actions that are sinful and wrong but never hate the person who does them. In Revelation chapter 2 verse 6, the Ephesians commendably hated 'the deeds of the Nicolaitanes', though it would have been wrong to hate the persons. When the Lord said, 'Jacob have I loved, but Esau have I hated', Rom. 9. 13, it is in a comparative way in relation to the great truth of election. Men will not find themselves in hell because God has ceased loving them, for He does not send the man to hell because he hates the man but because he hates his deeds. Each will be judged in relation to his deeds. That will, of course, add to the torment of sinners in hell and the lake of fire; God has not ceased loving them but His holiness and righteousness demanded that judgement for their deeds. Thus, it was not that God loved Esau less but that God hated the deeds that Esau took part in.

Three things that we know, 3. 16 – 4. 6

1. A past tense, 3. 16
    'Herein we have known the love of God.'

2. A future tense, 3. 19
    'And we shall know that we are of the truth.'

3. A present tense, 4. 6
>'Herein we do know the spirit of truth and the spirit of error.'

In verses 16 to 18, John is speaking of a past knowledge, the knowledge of experience contrasted with the knowledge of intuition. Verse 16 commences, 'Herein, we have perceived'. Then, in verses 19 to 23, John speaks of a future knowledge. Verse 19 might read, 'Hereby we shall know we are of the truth'. When John speaks in terms of the future, he is not thinking of eternity but of future experience. We shall know in future experience, if the Lord wills, that we are of the truth. Then, from verse 24 to chapter 4 verse 6, John speaks of a present knowledge, 'hereby we do know'.

3. 16 Hereby perceive we the love of God, because he laid down his life for us: and we ought to lay down our lives for the brethren.

The King James Version says '**perceive we**' but the Revised Version says 'know we'. It is in the perfect tense which indicates an action that has taken place in the past, the effect of which remains with us to the present day. In the King James Version, the words 'of God' are in italics; it could read, therefore, 'Hereby perceive we love'. 'Perceive' makes us understand that we know not just because we have heard but because we have understood. John is not speaking of the love of God as a person but of the love which is of God. Of course, it was not God but Christ who **laid down His life for us** and so the verse is to be understood as saying, 'Because He, that is Christ, laid down His life for us'. It is divine love in the heart of the Son of which John speaks. This is something we have known; the evidence, the conclusive proof, of divine love is that He laid down His life for us.

The expression '**laid down**' is an expression that is exclusive to John's writings. It is found in John chapter 10, verses 11, 15, 17 and 18.

'**He**' speaks of the greatness of the person who laid down His life for us; '**for us**' speaks of the unworthiness of the object. How this should touch our hearts! 'He' the worthy one, 'for us' the most unworthy ones, voluntarily laid down His life. Thus, it was a virtuous sacrifice made by so great a person; it was a voluntary sacrifice, in that He laid down His life; and being for us it was a vicarious sacrifice.

'**We ought to lay down our lives for the brethren**'. John loves to employ the word 'ought', which has the significance of a debt being involved. We should feel it as a debt, a bond and a duty to discharge that we lay down our lives for the brethren. The same word is found in chapter 2 verse 6, where we read, 'He that saith he abideth in him, ought himself also so to walk even as he walked'. The believer owes it as a debt to follow Christ's example. Again, in chapter 4 verse 11, 'we ought also to love one another'. In verse 8 of the third Epistle, 'we ought to receive such' as go forth in His name, taking nothing from the Gentiles. These are all debts that we owe as the children of God.

This verse is often misquoted. John does not say, 'hereby we have known love, because he laid down his life for us; therefore, we should lay down our lives for the brethren'. He does not use the word 'therefore' but simply says, 'and we ought to lay down our lives for the brethren'. The word 'therefore' would confine our obligation to a recognition of Christ's example; we might feel this as an obligation just because of Christ's example. In fact, what John is teaching is that we ought to lay down our lives for the brethren because of what the voluntary sacrifice has accomplished for us, which is that it has related each to the other as his brother. This voluntary sacrifice has brought us into this circle where we are the Lord's brethren and it is because of this that we ought to lay down our lives for all such. Epaphroditus, in Philippians chapter 2, is an example of one who was prepared to go that distance. He hazarded his life. The same thing is true in principle of Aquila and Priscilla, of whom the Apostle Paul says that they 'have for my life laid down their own necks', Rom. 16. 4. They did not die, of course, but were prepared to go that distance.

The challenge to each is, Would I be prepared to lay down my life for any particular brother or sister? One might say, 'Well, of course I would', knowing that there would probably be no call to do so, no test arising in that way. A little test is therefore presented in the next verse.

3. 17 **But whoso hath this world's good, and seeth his brother have need, and shutteth up his bowels of compassion from him, how dwelleth the love of God in him?**

In verse 16, our Saviour laid His life down for us on the cross and we ought to lay down our lives for the brethren. I should be prepared to die, if need be, for my brethren. It is possible that I will say that I will lay my life down for the brethren and yet despite having this world's good and seeing that my brother is in need do nothing about it. If so, how can I dare say I would lay down my life for my brethren? Once again it is not just a matter of saying; there is to be practical evidence of the reality of it.

'**Good**' simply means 'means of living'. It is the same word that occurs in chapter 2 verse 16, 'the pride of life', boasting in one's possessions. In this verse, it simply means 'subsistence', that which maintains our physical life in the world.

'**Seeth**' is a strong word and could be rendered 'beholdeth'; he fully beholds his brother has need. It is the same word in Hebrews chapter 7 verse 4, 'Now consider how great this man was'. We may sometimes rise to the occasion when an appeal is made but the thought in this verse is of not waiting for such a request. It is something we are prepared to do the moment we see it for ourselves; it is action upon seeing.

The thought expressed in '**shutteth up his bowels of compassion from him**' is very strong. Note that it is not just 'shutteth up his bowels' but 'shutteth up his bowels . . . from him'. Any feeling of compassion is excluded completely and there is involved a turning away from the one in need.

'**How dwelleth** [or, abideth] **the love of God in him?**' Notice that it is now the love of God, whereas in verse 1 it was the love of the Father. In verse 1, it is the love of the Father towards his children, but here it is the love of God which is more embracive, extending to the need of all

His creatures. How can that love be abiding in anyone who has behaved in this way? Romans chapter 12 verse 9 tells us that love is to be without dissimulation; unfeigned and without hypocrisy. 'Seeing ye have purified your souls in obeying the truth through the Spirit unto unfeigned love of the brethren, see that ye love one another with a pure heart fervently' is the language of 1 Peter chapter 1 verse 22. The idea of hypocritical love is common in the New Testament; in relation to love we can be guilty of hypocrisy and insincerity.

3. 18   My little children, let us not love in word, neither in tongue; but in deed and in truth.

'**Little children**', as we have already observed, is the diminutive of affection, 'dear children'. John is not addressing himself to the infants but to all in the family; fathers, young men and infants.

'**Let us not love in** [with] **word, neither in** [with the] **tongue**'. It is important to notice that the word 'tongue' is emphasized here because the tongue is the medium for the profession of love. Loving with word is loving theoretically, in the mind, but loving with the tongue is to profess love and perhaps not even to have it in the mind. It is possible to say plenty about loving one another and it be all theoretical. However, we sometimes go further and profess it, but, says John, let us love in '**deed and in truth**'. 'In deed' contrasts with 'in theory'; 'in truth' is instead of 'in mere profession', or hypocritical confession.

3. 19   And hereby we know that we are of the truth, and shall assure our hearts before him.

The future tense is employed, '**And hereby we** [shall] **know that we are of the truth**'. If we love in deed and in truth, we shall know, in our Christian experience, that we are of the truth. The force of the preposition in '**of the truth**' (*ek*, which means 'out of') is that our living as children of God is regulated by the truth and characterized by truthfulness. Then we '**shall assure**', or persuade, '**our hearts before him**', or in His presence, because of our sincerity and by our living by the truth. It is not, of course, persuading ourselves as to our salvation;

rather, it is the matter of boldness in His presence because our life is in the character of God, being utterly sincere.

The idea of asking and receiving, v. 22, involves His presence now, but '**shall**' is in respect of future Christian experience in the matter of prayer. There is nothing that condemns us more than insincerity in His presence when we pray.

The two little words '**before him**' are also used in chapter 2 verse 28, where we read, 'And now, little children, abide in him; that, when he shall appear, we may have confidence, and not be ashamed before him at his coming'. That verse is in relation to the Judgement Seat of Christ.

3. 20   For if our heart condemn us, God is greater than our heart, and knoweth all things.

'**Our heart**' will **condemn us**, or convict us, in God's presence by reason of insincerity in loving in word and in tongue. We are not, then, at home in God's presence, our communion is disturbed and we are not able to express ourselves with confidence in prayer. Our insincerity rebukes us and the Spirit of God reminds us of our need of self-judgement. John says that in that event '**God is greater than our heart, and knoweth all things**'. This is not a word of consolation but is, in fact, very searching and solemn. John is saying, 'If our heart condemn us, how much more also God, for God is greater than our heart and he knoweth all things'. God knows more than we know in the matter of this insincerity of loving in word and in tongue but not in deed and in truth.

3. 21   Beloved, if our heart condemn us not, then have we confidence toward God.

Our heart does not **condemn us** if we are sincere, with the result that we have undisturbed communion, not being either rebuked or occupied with the need of self-judgement. The result of this is seen in verse 22.

Confidence in God is a general attitude, but here '**confidence toward God**' is a particular experience in the matter of prayer. On a very practical note, all will know that if we are guilty of insincerity there is nothing that condemns us more in the presence of God when we pray.

3.22 And whatsoever we ask, we receive of him, because we keep his commandments, and do those things that are pleasing in his sight.

Here, we have the great result of sincerity, namely answered prayer. Notice the two expressions, '**we ask**' and '**we receive**'. The secret of answered prayer is the heart being uncondemned in God's presence because of sincerity, and therefore being in touch with God. If we are in touch with God, then we ask according to His will. Thus, John gives us the secret of answered prayer; it is obedience to God in keeping **His commandments**. We are then well-pleasing in His sight, delighting God, doing the things that please Him.

3.23 And this is his commandment, That we should believe on the name of his Son Jesus Christ, and love one another, as he gave us commandment.

If it is correct to differentiate between God and His Son in this verse, then there are two commandments. '**And this is his commandment**' is, of course, the commandment of God, for John is continuing what he has been teaching in the preceding verses. In verse 20, 'God is greater than our heart'; in verse 21, 'we have confidence towards God'; in verse 22, 'whatsoever we ask we receive from God'. Now, in verse 23, 'this is his commandment'.

The verse ends with '**as he gave us commandment**'. This commandment to love one another is, of course, the commandment of the Son of God; in John chapter 13 verse 34, He spoke of this as 'a new commandment'.

The commandment that God gave was that we should believe on the name of His Son, Jesus Christ; and the commandment to love one another is connected with the Son of God. These two matters of faith and love are found together repeatedly in the New Testament. In

Ephesians chapter 1 verse 15, the apostle speaks of their 'faith in the Lord Jesus, and love unto all the saints'. In Galatians chapter 5 verse 6, he speaks of 'faith which worketh by love'.

It is an important matter to note that this verse should read, 'And this is his commandment that we **believe the name** of his Son, Jesus Christ' and not 'that we should believe on the name of his Son, Jesus Christ'. There is no preposition and so it does not read 'on'. Of course, John speaks both in the Gospel and in this Epistle of believing on the Son. He says in chapter 5 verse 13, 'These things have I written unto you that believe on the name of the Son of God; that ye may know that ye have eternal life, and that ye may believe on the name of the Son of God'. In John chapter 1 verse 12, he says, 'But as many as received him, to them gave he power to become the sons of God, even to them that believe on his name'. But here it is not believing 'on' the name, nor is it believing 'in' the name; it is 'believing the name'. Believing 'on the name' signifies that the person is the object of trust but 'believing the name' is to believe all that that name signifies and all that that name reveals. The name is here brought before us in wondrous fullness. The commandment is that we believe the name of 'his Son', which indicates His deity; 'Jesus', which indicates His humanity; and 'Christ', which speaks of His mission as the anointed one.

In chapter 5 verse 13, believing 'on the name of the Son of God' is connected with the present possession of eternal life, but what we have here is something in advance of that, in that it is believing the name itself and all that name reveals. John chapter 5 verse 24 is often misquoted. It does not say that hearing the Son and believing on God gives eternal life; it should read, 'he that heareth my word, and believeth him that sent me, hath everlasting life'. It speaks of believing God's record concerning the Son. These are important matters to differentiate. Paul said in Acts chapter 27 verse 25, 'I believe God', but it is not believing God that initially brings us salvation. When Peter says, in 1 Peter chapter 1 verse 21, 'who by him do believe in God' the proper rendering is, 'who by him have become believers in God'. It is not the initial act of faith but what characterizes the Christian in contrast to those who do not believe in God. When it is the act of faith bringing salvation, it is believing in the person of God's Son; He is the object of faith.

To believe the name is a **commandment**, which is very important. There is no option in this matter. This rules out the doctrine of, say, the so-called Jehovah's Witnesses, who do not believe the name of His Son with all that it involves as to His deity.

Then, there is the **commandment** from His Son, which is to love one another. Love is here allied to, and inseparable from, believing. In verse 22, the reference is to God's commandments, an expression which embraces all that is in His word that we have to obey; but in verse 23 it is only one of God's commandments. This is the new commandment of chapter 2 verse 8 and of John chapter 13 verse 34. The new commandment is to love with that love which was exemplified in Christ: 'that ye love one another; as I have loved you'. In the Old Testament the commandment was to love one's neighbour as one's self, but the new commandment gives to this matter of loving a greater motive and the noblest example, as Christ has loved us.

We have to be commanded to love because of the flesh in each one of us, which makes us envious and suspicious of each other. If we do not love one another there is involved, solemnly, disobedience to a divine command. Loving one another, then, is not optional. It is, of course, one of the evidences of the new birth, and here it is brought before us as a divine command.

This is divine love. Peter says, in 2 Peter chapter 1 verse 7, that we are to add 'to brotherly kindness, charity'. Charity, or love, is something higher than even brotherly kindness or brotherly love. It is divine love operating in the heart that enables us to love one another despite the fact that a brother or sister might perhaps irritate or say something to offend. After all, we have to remember that God loved each one of us when we were most unlovable.

3. 24 And he that keepeth his commandments dwelleth in him, and he in him. And hereby we know that he abideth in us, by the Spirit which he hath given us.

Here, the child of God is abiding in God and God is abiding in him. This is not simply being in God and God being in His child, but it is the thought of abiding as being constantly at home and enjoying communion. It is mutual enjoyment of communion between the child and his God.

There are conditions for this, which involve obedience in keeping His **commandments**. These two things are emphasized by John in his Epistle.[4] John places great stress on obedience.

In the latter half of verse 24, which finishes this section, John is speaking about present knowledge: 'hereby we know that he abideth in us, by the Spirit which he hath given us'. John is saying that we know that God has made His home in our hearts, that He abideth in us, **by the Spirit** He gave to us.

'By' is not 'because of' the Spirit; the Greek word is *ek* which is 'out of'. We know that God abides in us by the working of the Spirit of God in our hearts and lives. John is not here speaking only of the gift of the indwelling Spirit but of the ministry and power of the Spirit of God in our lives.

He gave the Spirit to all of us the moment we believed. There is no such thing as the believer not having the Spirit of God; everyone, upon believing, receives the Holy Spirit.

---

[4] See: 2. 3; 3. 22, 24; 5. 3.

Chapter 4

Three things that we know (continued), 4. 1-6

Having spoken of the Spirit given to us in chapter 3 verse 24, the apostle now goes on to speak about evil spirits, in verses 1 to 6. He is speaking of influences that are at work, and the great unseen spiritual conflict in this world against Christ and against the children of God. The important expression 'in the world' occurs three times in this section, vv. 1, 3 and 4.

Notice the contrasts that John brings before us in this remarkable section. If, in chapter 3 verse 24, John tells us that God has given the Holy Spirit, he speaks, in chapter 4 verse 3, of the devil having sent spirits into the world. These spirits are not of God, v. 3; they advance the principle of antichrist.

Then, notice that in verse 6, Christ has sent His apostles, and John says of them, 'we are of God'. 'He that knoweth God heareth us' refers to the apostles that Christ has sent into the world, who are of God. In contrast, in verse 1, the devil has sent false prophets into the world 'because many false prophets are gone out into the world'. There are, then, false prophets in contrast to the apostles who are of God.

Then, in verse 2, John says of the Holy Spirit that He is the Spirit of God. In verse 2, He confesses Jesus Christ; in verse 4, He is greater than the devil; in verse 6, He is the Spirit of truth. By way of contrast, John says, in verse 3, that the evil spirits are not of God, and they confess not that Jesus Christ is come in the flesh; and, in verse 6, they are characterized by the spirit of error.

Furthermore, the apostles are of God, v. 6, but these false prophets who have gone out into the world, v. 5, are of the world, and speak of the world, and the world hears them.

4. 1 Beloved, believe not every spirit, but try the spirits whether they are of God: because many false prophets are gone out into the world.

The child of God must not **believe every spirit** but, rather, **try the spirits**. John tells us the twofold test in this matter of trying, or proving, every spirit, which can be easily remembered. Firstly, we test them in respect of the person of Christ; secondly, we test them in relation to the word of God. In verses 2 and 3, the test is whether or not they confess Jesus Christ. This puts every spirit to the test, 'what think ye of Christ?' The second test, in verse 6, is the word of God and involves their attitude and response to apostolic teaching. 'He that knoweth God heareth us; he that is not of God heareth not us'.

We have around us today many evil, false cults. The principle of antichrist is abroad and increasing daily. Put everyone to this test, 'What think ye of Christ?' Secondly, what do you think of apostolic teaching? If they fall down on either or both of these, they are advancing the principle of antichrist.

In 1 Corinthians chapter 12, one of the gifts that is mentioned is the discerning of spirits. This particular gift is not what we have here. What John is speaking of here is the exercise that belongs to every child of God. Obviously, the spirits must operate through human agencies, as verse 2 makes clear; the spirits can only confess through human agencies. We test whatever confession we hear by any man and by doing this we test the spirit that has prompted this confession.

False prophets are 'imitation prophets'. They believe, possibly, in His incarnation, but they do not confess or believe the implications of it. The worst form of wrong doctrine is that which contains a measure of truth. It is very remarkable to observe that false prophets are spoken of quite frequently in the New Testament. In Matthew chapter 7 verse 15, they 'come to you in sheep's clothing, but inwardly they are ravening wolves'. In Matthew chapter 24 verse 11, 'many false prophets shall rise, and shall deceive many'. In Mark chapter 13 verse 22, 'false Christs and false prophets shall rise, and shall shew signs and wonders, to deceive, if it were possible, even the elect'. Thus, they are in sheep's clothing, guilty of deception and are even capable of showing signs and wonders. It is necessary to understand that these false prophets are capable of exercising certain spiritual powers, so as to deceive. People today are very easily influenced by what professes to be a miracle and, apparently, a great sign, perhaps of miraculous healing or some other thing. It is time that we realized that miracles are no evidence of the right or wrong with any particular teaching.

'**Many false prophets are gone out into the world**' is an advance on chapter 2 verse 19, where many antichrists 'went out from us'. Here, it is not them going out from us but going out into the world. This is now their sphere of operation.

4. 2 Hereby know ye the Spirit of God: Every spirit that confesseth that Jesus Christ is come in the flesh is of God:

The verse should read, 'Every spirit that confesseth Jesus Christ'. The second 'that' is omitted, as is the first 'is'. The inclusion of the words would give the wrong idea; what would be emphasized is what was an historical fact which is believed by many who are not of God. The omission of the words signifies that confessing has tremendous implications connected with this fact; it is confessing **Jesus Christ come in flesh**.

No mere man came in the flesh; we were born but He came. That involves His deity and the fact that He came into manhood. One who existed eternally as God has stepped into manhood. The word is not 'came' but 'come', which involves the purpose of His coming which was to make atonement and to die for us. Thus, this is not the confession of a fact but the confession of His deity and the purpose for which He came.

The best that could be said of John the Baptist, the greatest of the prophets, was that 'There was a man sent from God, whose name was John', John 1.6. He was sent but Jesus came. John the Baptist was born supernaturally but not without precedent, for Isaac was born in exactly the same way, from a dead womb. Jesus' conception was not just supernatural but it was divine as He was conceived of the Spirit of God. John the Baptist was not born without the agency of man, unlike Jesus. These are tremendously important matters and anyone who would disagree has the spirit of antichrist.

There were three 'sendings forth' of the dove from the ark. The first time it came back, speaking of the operation of the Spirit in the Old Testament; there was nothing but carnage, nothing for the heart of God. The second time it came back with the olive leaf, that which speaks of that which was introduced with Christ. The third time it did not come back at all. The third time refers to the millennial reign; He will not come back as He will be poured out upon all flesh. The Spirit is thus connected in a special way to the advent and work of Christ in this world.

In this connection, it is very interesting to observe the involvement of the triune God in His incarnation, His entry into public service and His death at Calvary. At His incarnation God prepared His body, Heb. 10. 7. In Luke chapter 1 verse 35, that body was conceived by the Holy Spirit. In John chapter 1, there is the activity of the Son: 'the word became flesh', John 1. 14. Thirty years later, at His baptism, the Lord comes up out of the water in His character as the Lamb of God, the Spirit descends like a dove and the voice of the Father is heard to say, 'Thou art my beloved Son'. Then, last of all, He, through an eternal Spirit, offered himself without spot unto God, Heb. 9. 14. These are the three important epochs; His incarnation, His moving into public service and His death at Calvary.

The dove speaks of gentleness; the Spirit of God descending and abiding upon Him as a dove speaks of complete complacency. There was nothing in Christ or about Him that could hinder the dove descending in this gentle character and abiding on Him. It speaks of His utter holiness.

4. 3 **And every spirit that confesseth not that Jesus Christ is come in the flesh is not of God: and this is that spirit of antichrist, whereof ye have heard that it should come; and even now already is it in the world.**

It should read 'the Jesus', the **Jesus** of whom John has been speaking, making unnecessary the repetition of 'Christ come in the flesh'. This proves that this is the truth of the person and not just His incarnation as an historical fact.

Notice it does not say, 'And every spirit that knoweth not the Jesus'; it is **'confesseth not'**. Demons know the truth of His person but they would not confess it, because confession involves believing. 'Confesseth not' is not merely their silence on the matter but rather the fact that they are not prepared to confess the truth that is involved in Jesus Christ come in the flesh. One said, 'I know thee who thou art; the Holy One of God', Luke 4. 34, which is a declaration of truth as to His person but not a confession of the truth of Jesus Christ come in flesh. The word to 'confess' is a compound of two words meaning 'to speak together'. Confession is agreeing with God as to what He has said in His word regarding the person of His Son, with the context here being Jesus Christ come in the flesh, involving His humanity, deity and the purpose for which He came.

Such a spirit **'is not of God'** as to its origin. In chapter 3 verse 10, John says, 'whosoever doeth not righteousness is not of God', which is the same expression as here. There the context is that wrong conduct is evidence that the individual is not of God but here it is wrong doctrine that is an evidence that this is not of God. Thus, wrong conduct and wrong doctrine are two things that prove anything as not being of God.

'This is that spirit of antichrist.' 'Spirit' is in italics, not being expressed in the Greek. It actually reads, 'this is the of antichrist'. What John is speaking of here is the principle of antichrist. In the first part of the verse, the spirit that confesseth not Jesus Christ come in flesh is not of God, but now John adds that this is the principle of antichrist. The principle of antichrist is against Christ and **even now already is it in the world**. The spirit of antichrist denies His deity, the import of His incarnation and the purpose for which He came, to die for our sins.

'Whereof ye have heard that it should come' is the prediction; **'and even now already is it in the world'** is the fulfilment of the prediction.

That is in line with the teaching of 2 Thessalonians chapter 2 verse 7 which says, 'For the mystery of iniquity doth already work'. The lawless one is not yet manifested, and will not be until after our Lord comes, but the mystery of lawlessness already works.

4. 4   Ye are of God, little children, and have overcome them: because greater is he that is in you, than he that is in the world.

This is addressed to all God's family. **'Ye'** is emphatic; it is in contrast to the false prophets. In chapter 3 verse 1, John says, 'Behold, what manner of love the Father hath bestowed upon us, that we should be called the sons of God'. However, this is not quite the same. We are called the children of God in chapter 3 verse 1, but here John says, **'ye are of God, little children'**. This does not just mean that we are the children of God as those who are born of God but it signifies that we have a link with God; not only born of God but to those who are 'little children' God is the source of all their blessing.

'**And have overcome them**'. 'Them' is masculine and refers to the false prophets, who were the devil's agents. In chapter 2 verse 14, John speaks of the young men who have overcome the evil one; they did this because they were strong and the word of God was abiding in them. However, he is now referring to all the children in God's family. They have overcome not just the evil one but the false prophets '**because greater is he that is in you, than he that is in the world**'. This refers to the Holy Spirit. The young men overcome because of the word of God abiding in them, but the little children overcome because of the Holy Spirit within each of them. This speaks of the omnipresence of the Holy Spirit.

Notice that John says, 'Ye are of God, little children, and have overcome them'. Notice also that it is 'he' that is in the world' not 'them' that are in the world. You have overcome 'them', the false prophets; but he that is in the world is the devil himself, for he is the authority and power above and behind the evil spirits that operate in the false prophets.

Thus, in this verse it is not just the false teachers that are in the world but the devil is in the world.

There is an important point here. The Holy Spirit is in us individually but when it comes to the devil it does not say that he is in the false prophets. Rather, his evil spirits are in the false prophets, for although the Holy Spirit is omnipresent the devil is not. Therefore, he has to use multitudinous evil spirits in his false prophets and antichrists that are abroad. As has often been pointed out, there is one devil but many demons. The devil is not omnipresent and he uses his demons, his evil spirits.

4. 5 They are of the world: therefore speak they of the world, and the world heareth them.

'**They**' is emphatic; they are out of the world. When John says '**they are of the world**' he means that they are of this world system, which is apart from God and hostile to Him; the world is their source of teaching. John has already said something about the world in chapter 2 verse 16, where he says, 'For all that is in the world, the lust of the flesh, and the lust of the eyes, and the pride of life, is not of the Father, but is of the world'. The Lord Jesus said to his own in John chapter 15 verse 19, 'If ye were of the world, the world would love his own; but because ye are not of the world, but I have chosen you out of the world, therefore the world hateth you'. They are all of this world system and for this reason speak they of the world.

'**Therefore speak they of the world**' does not mean they speak about or concerning the world but that this world system, that is apart from God and hostile towards Him, is the source of their speaking. The source of their speaking is Satan's world.

'**The world heareth them**' is the world apart from God and without His Spirit.

4. 6 **We are of God: he that knoweth God heareth us; he that is not of God heareth not us. Hereby know we the spirit of truth, and the spirit of error.**

In verse 4, John says, 'ye are of God' but now he says, '**we are of God**'. 'We' refers to the apostles, but 'ye' refers to all the family, so that both the apostles and all the family were of God.

'**He that knoweth God heareth us**'. Every child of God has eternal life, knows God and hears the doctrine of the apostles. This is an important matter. The apostles had an important role in the early days of the church. In 1 John chapter 1, there is the fellowship of the apostles; they declared what they saw and heard so that we might have fellowship with them. Here, it is the doctrine of the apostles, which is so important to observe. The teaching of 1 Corinthians chapter 2 verse 13, when Paul says, 'we speak, not in the words which man's wisdom teacheth, but which the Holy Ghost teacheth', does not apply to every servant of God. No servant of God, however spiritual, would claim that every word that he spoke was a word that the Spirit gave him. This is apostolic. Having the gift of the word of wisdom, and the gift of the word of knowledge, and their inspiration, their oral ministry had this character to which that verse refers. Thus, Paul could say in 1 Corinthians chapter 14 verse 37, 'If any man think himself to be a prophet, or spiritual, let him acknowledge that the things that I write unto you are the commandments of the Lord'.

Notice that John does not say, 'he that knoweth not God' but '**he that is not of God**'; only those who know God are 'of God'.

Whether the word of God is accepted or not is the second part of the twofold test by which we try every spirit. '**Hereby know we the spirit of truth, and the spirit of the error**' means that the apostles knew the spirit of truth and the spirit of error from those who heard and those who did not hear.

Three things about the love of God, 4. 7 – 5. 3

The triad of truth in this section has to do with love.

1. The love of God toward us, vv. 7-11.
2. The love of God perfected in us, vv. 12-16.
3. The love of God perfected with us, v. 17 – 5. 3.

With regard to verses 7 to 11, the language of verse 9 is, 'In this was manifested the love of God toward us'. The thought here is of the love of God manifested in our case, which is confirmed in verse 10. This love was expressed toward us **as sinners**, who were dead, v. 9, and guilty, v. 10. He sent his Son as the propitiation for our sins not because we were dead and in need of life, as in verse 9, but because we were guilty and needed forgiveness. In this section, John is dealing with the source of love and so speaks of God alone.

Then, with regard to verses 12 to 16, the language of verse 12 is, 'If we love one another, God dwelleth in us, and his love is perfected in us'. The love of God is perfected in us **as children** by God dwelling in us by the Spirit, v. 13.

Then, with regard to chapter 4 verse 17 to chapter 5 verse 3, it is the love of God perfected with us, v. 17. When the love of God is made perfect with us **as His creatures**, we are assured of boldness in the future day of judgement. This is the judgement of God in relation to his creatures. John now introduces not the Spirit but the Son of God, 'as he [the Son of God] is, so are we in this world'.

The first six verses of chapter 4 form a digression in which John calls upon us to try the spirits. From chapter 4 verse 7 to chapter 5 verse 3, John resumes the theme of love that he has been developing in chapter 3 verses 11 to 23, although he makes a different approach.

In chapter 3 verse 11, John speaks of the message that they had heard from the beginning, that they should love one another. He makes the basis of this appeal the sacrifice of Christ Himself. Thus, he says in verse

16, 'Hereby perceive we the love of God, because he laid down his life for us; and we ought to lay down our lives for the brethren'. Not only does he make this the basis of his appeal but he issues a challenge, in verse 16, to God's children based on that sacrifice. The challenge is that 'we ought to lay down our lives for the brethren'. John is, in that section, also enjoining upon us that our love ought to be sincere, loving not merely in word and tongue but in deed and in truth, v. 18. Sincere love gives us boldness toward God now, in prayer, and whatsoever we ask we receive of him, v. 22.

Now, in chapter 4 verse 7, John says, 'Beloved let us love one another', but the basis of John's appeal in this section is not the sacrifice of Christ but the fact that God sent His Son, v. 9. He says in verse 11, 'Beloved, if God so loved us, we ought also to love one another'. If God loved us to such an extent as to send His Son, then we ought also to love one another. Also, in the previous section, John speaks in chapter 3 of the necessity of sincere love, which gives boldness, but in this section John speaks of perfect love, which also gives us boldness, v. 17, in the future day of judgement. Accordingly, sincere love gives us boldness in God's presence as we pray to Him now, but perfect love gives us boldness in regard to the future day of judgement.

These are very fine distinctions but tremendously important to observe. Observe, too, that both of these sections conclude with a commandment. Thus, though they are different they are strikingly similar, and both conclude with a commandment, 3. 23; 4. 21.

4. 7   Beloved, let us love one another: for love is of God; and every one that loveth is born of God, and knoweth God.

John always uses **'beloved'** in the sense of an appeal. He is addressing God's children as those who are not just beloved of God but also beloved by John himself. It is, of course, the love of God in the heart of John that makes him look upon them as his beloved. It is quite remarkable how often in the Epistles the writers address the people of God as 'beloved'. It is an expression that speaks of sanctified affection and ought to be true of us in our attitude and relationship with all God's people. This is love in the circle of the family of God, all who have been born of God. It was to the Corinthian believers, with all their disorder and disarray, that Paul said, 'Therefore, my beloved brethren, be ye stedfast, unmovable, always abounding in the work of the Lord', 1 Cor. 15. 58.

The first love of Revelation chapter 2 is linked by some with the Ephesian letter, relating it to the love for all the saints. It is better understood that first love is love toward Christ, not being first in terms of time but in terms of degree. It indicates that the Lord rightly expects that we maintain our love towards him at its highest level at all times. He deserves nothing less than that. There is, of course, a test to that; 'if ye love me, keep my commandments, John 14. 15. When we fail to be obedient to His word we are leaving our first love towards Christ.

The reason why we must love one another is because **love is of God**. There can be no true, pure and unselfish love that does not have its source in God. This is something far higher than philanthropy, which is the love of man toward man on the plane of mankind. Even the love for a father, or a son, is loving in the realm and within the sphere of men but what John speaks of here is *agape,* divine love, a love which is far higher, being pure, unselfish and utterly sincere.

Further, '**everyone that loveth is born of God**'; or, 'everyone that loveth hath been begotten of God'. Everyone who loves in purity, in fidelity and with no selfish interest has been begotten of God. John is reasoning that if love is of God, in that it is His nature, then whoever is begotten of Him partakes of His nature. There can be no pure and sincere love, no matter what the object might be, unless one has been begotten of God.

4. 8   He that loveth not knoweth not God; for God is love.

John employs the past tense, 'He that loveth not knew not God'. This is rather amazing in that the antithesis to what is stated in verse 7 should have been 'he that loveth not hath not been begotten of God'. John rather says, 'he that loveth not never at any time came to know God'. Observe that it is not here knowing about God but about knowing God intimately in the sense of possessing eternal life. 'This is life eternal, that they might know thee the only true God, and Jesus Christ, whom thou hast sent', John 17. 3. The theme of this section is '**God is love**', whereas in chapter 1 it was 'God is light'.

God is light as to His nature, something that is true of Him even supposing there was never any darkness. The expression '**God is love**' also speaks of His nature and He is love whether or not there is an object in which He would express His love. In verse 9, however, there is the expression of it, 'in this was manifested the love of God'.

4. 9   In this was manifested the love of God toward us, because that God sent his only begotten Son into the world, that we might live through him.

In this was manifested the love of God **toward us**, or 'in our case'. If, in verse 8, John says that God is love, in verse 9 he speaks of the love of God manifested toward us. In verse 16, he speaks of the love that God has to us, or the love that God has in connection with us.

His love was **manifested** 'because God hath sent his only begotten Son into the world, that we might live through him'. The expression '**his only begotten Son**' is an expression that belongs exclusively to John's writings. God sent Him; the tense is 'hath' sent 'his only begotten Son into the world'. Notice the two expressions, 'His only begotten Son' and 'into this world'. God's unique Son was sent into a world that was hostile and opposed to God. God sent His only begotten Son into the world to do something that could not have been done in heaven, or from heaven but only in the world. How wondrous was God's love that He sent His unique Son into such a world as this, having in view that we might live through Him; that we might have life from the dead through the Son.

Perhaps the highest example of paternal love was between Abraham and Isaac. God said, 'Take now thy son, thine only Isaac whom thou lovest', Gen. 22. 2. This was a tremendous cost to the heart of a man like Abraham. Here, however, it is not a human heart but the heart of the eternal God sending not an Isaac but His unique Son. A man's or a woman's dearest child is just like a stranger to them compared with the exceeding dearness of God's unique Son to His heart and yet it was in this sending of His Son that there was manifested the love of God toward us. The question arises as to why God should love people like us, for none deserved that God should manifest His love toward us in such a way. He sent one who was unique, His only begotten Son, into a world like this and we shall never know what it meant for Him to be in such a world, so hostile to God.

God's love is expressed as being toward 'us', not toward 'all men'. However, the love of God is towards the whole world, John 3. 16. The love of the Father is towards His children, 1 John 3. 1. The love of Christ is towards His church, Eph. 5. 25. The love of the Son is towards the individual believer, Gal. 2. 20. In this verse, while it is true that the love of God extends to all men, John is thinking here of applying the message to those who have responded and the response that ought to be produced in their heart, v. 11.

God sent His Son **that we might live**. That means we were spiritually dead. Just as corpses are loathsome to the heart of any man or woman, and so we bury them out of sight, men who are spiritual corpses are just as loathsome to the heart of a holy God. Yet, for those who were dead, and who deserved only to be buried out of God's sight, God sent into the world His unique Son that we might have life **through Him**. This idea of life through Him is very interesting. The expression could mean either that we have life through His work at the place called Calvary or that life can come to us instrumentally through Him today. Both of these are true. In Romans chapter 5 verse 21, Paul speaks of grace reigning through righteousness unto eternal life through Jesus Christ our Lord. This is through His sacrifice at Calvary and only because of that sacrifice could life come to us through Him. However, it also comes to us through Him instrumentally, 'the Son quickeneth whom he will', John 5. 21.

God gives to all the offer of life but the experience of living is based upon appropriation. The father said of the prodigal that his son was lost and is found but he then said that he was dead and now is alive again. In the far country he was not dead physically, for he was devouring his living with harlots, but, as far as his father was concerned, he was dead. People living in pleasure and in sin are dead before God and in need of this life.

Verses 9 and 10 have to be taken together. In verse 9, we were dead and needed life; in verse 10, we were guilty and propitiation was needed. Life is something we required but propitiation is something God required. In the Gospels, it is God's side first; in the Epistles, it is man's side first. That is why, in John chapter 19 verse 34, the order is blood and water but in John's first Epistle it is water and blood; water, verse 9, for life, and blood, verse 10, for propitiation.

In John chapter 3 verse 16, God gave, but here it is 'God sent'. There is, of course, a difference between God 'giving' and God 'sending'. God 'giving' is connected with the heart of God, whilst God 'sending' is connected with the hand of God, the authority of God, that we might live. It is also important to observe, in verse 9, that it is 'hath sent', the perfect tense involving something that God did in the past but with permanent results that remain with us, namely that we might live.

4. 10   Herein is love, not that we loved God, but that he loved us, and sent his Son to be the propitiation for our sins.

'**Sent**' is in the aorist tense, stating a fact once and for all accomplished. This is because it is to do with the propitiation for our sins, something that does not need repeating. It involves the love that is inherent in God's nature. If John had merely said, '**Herein is love**' it might have meant, 'Herein is the only expression of love', namely that God sent His Son to be the propitiation for our sins. God surrounds us with so many expressions of his love; homes to live in, friends to comfort, beds to lie upon, constant preservation from danger. John says, in fact, 'Herein is **the** love' before which every other expression of divine love toward us fades away and recedes, even as the shining of the sun extinguishes the stars. When we think of the **the** love in the sending of His Son it is the love of God in all its fullness.

Love that no thought can reach,

> Love that no tongue can teach,
> No love like thine.
>
> [THOMAS KELLY]

Notice that it is '**not that we**' and '**but that he**'. This is tremendously important and a fount of truth is involved in these two statements. God's love was first in time and since God's love toward us was first in time it was love that was despite us. Our love was in return for God's love. Therefore, our love to God was because of God's love to us. God 'is rich in mercy, for his great love wherewith he loved us', Eph. 2. 4.

It is the Son sent as the **propitiation for our sins**. In chapter 2 verse 2, He is Himself 'the propitiation for our sins', in all the good of an accomplished work at the place called Calvary and having left the world, being now on heaven's throne. Here, however, it is the sending of His Son into this world, to be the propitiation for our sins.

Propitiation for sins is the satisfaction of divine justice in respect of its claim against sins. It is associated with the blood of Christ. Let us remember that when He shed His blood the claims of divine justice, the claims of the throne of God, in respect of the sins of the whole world were completely satisfied. The effect of it is, judicially, the removal of God's displeasure because of sin, though the sin of the individual sinner is not judicially removed until he believes.

4. 11 Beloved, if God so loved us, we ought also to love one another.

The word '**beloved**' occurs again, for the sixth and last time in this Epistle. The expression, '**God so loved us**' relates to what has been taught in verses 9 and 10. God so loved us as to send His only begotten Son.

Notice the word '**also**'. We ought, as well as God, to love one another and to love our brethren despite what they might do and say against us. John speaks of this matter of loving one another as a new commandment. To fail to love is disobedience toward a commandment.

God loved us despite our being dead and guilty, but it was a righteous love, that had taken into account our condition.

In his Gospel, John speaks of himself five times over as 'the disciple whom Jesus loved'. This is how he speaks of himself, never referring to himself by name. In the second Epistle by John, he speaks of himself as an elder. In the book of Revelation, he speaks of himself as a brother. When John speaks of himself as the disciple whom Jesus loved, he is not saying that Jesus loved him more than others. Such would be the thought of Peter when he said, 'Though all men shall be offended because of thee, yet will I never be offended', Matt. 26. 33. John simply appreciated the fact that Jesus loved him. We could go a long way living in the enjoyment of the fact that we are loved of Him.

4. 12   No man hath seen God at any time. If we love one another, God dwelleth in us, and his love is perfected in us.

In verses 12 to 16, there is another aspect of this love, the love of God perfected in us.

No man has **beheld God** at any time, yet there was one here who had declared Him, His only begotten Son. 'No man hath seen God at any time; the only begotten Son, which is in the bosom of the father, He hath declared him', John 1. 18. The only begotten Son, who declared God when He was here, has now gone back to heaven and can no longer be seen; but if we love one another, **God dwelleth in us** and can be seen in us.

Loving one another is not just the evidence of God abiding in us but it is necessary to the enjoyment of it. And His love '**hath been perfected in us**'. God's love cannot be improved; it is perfect. This means that His love toward us has reached its desired end as far as we are concerned in that we love one another, and God Himself has found a home in our hearts. There is another way in this Epistle in which the love of God is perfected. 'But whoso keepeth his word, in him verily is the love of God perfected; hereby know we that we are in him', 2. 5. By obedience, the love of God reaches its desired end in us. There are, therefore, two ways in which His love can be perfected, by our obedience to His word and in the matter of our loving one another.

4. 13 Hereby know we that we dwell in him, and he in us, because he hath given us of his Spirit.

John is now reverting to the same subject that he has been dealing with in verses 9 and 10. There, it was to teach us to love one another, but here, it is from the standpoint that we ourselves might dwell in the enjoyment of divine love and of what is ours by divine grace. We know that '**we dwell in him**' and we know this because '**he hath given us of his Spirit**'. It is not 'He has given us his Spirit' but 'he hath given us of his Spirit'; not a portion of it but 'out of' His Spirit as the source by which this communion is enjoyed. It is by the Spirit's power in our lives. Accordingly, John is not speaking merely of the possession of the Spirit who has been given to us but of the Spirit as the power to know and enjoy God in us, and we in God. The same Spirit, so to speak, is shared wonderfully by God and us. See also the teaching of chapter 3 verse 24.

4. 14 And we have seen and do testify that the Father sent the Son to be the Saviour of the world.

'**We**' refers to the apostles, who had beheld and had scrutinized the Son. No man has seen God, v. 12, but we have seen the Son, and, having seen the Son, we do **testify** that the Father sent the Son as the Saviour of the world.

'**The Saviour of the world**' is an expression used exclusively by John. Pharaoh called Joseph's name Zaphnath-paaneah, which has a twofold significance. It means 'a revealer of secrets' and 'the saviour of the world'. Joseph revealed the secrets of the two in prison and then became the saviour of the world. That is what Christ was in John chapter 4; He revealed to the woman at the well the secrets of her heart when He said, 'Thou hast had five husbands', but then manifested Himself to the Samaritans as the Saviour of the world. John writes for the world, a word which occurs seventy-two times in his Gospel.

4. 15 Whosoever shall confess that Jesus is the Son of God, God dwelleth in him, and he in God.

The word '**confess**' is a compound of two words and has the force of 'to agree with'. It is agreeing with God in what He has to say about His Son. '**Jesus**' is His manhood; '**the Son of God**' is His deity.

When John speaks in terms of what 'we know', 3. 24, he introduces the thought of the indwelling Spirit of God; we know by reason of the Spirit of God who indwells us and the power of the Spirit of God in our lives. Here, however, the word is '**whosoever**'; and it is a matter of confession. We know in ourselves by the power of the indwelling Spirit in our lives but we can only tell if others believe by their confession. It is because John has been speaking about the Son in verse 14 that he speaks about confessing that Jesus is the Son of God in verse 15. This confession involves the fact that the Father sent one who was the Son to be the Saviour of the world.

4. 16 And we have known and believed the love that God hath to us. God is love; and he that dwelleth in love dwelleth in God, and God in him.

'We' in verse 14 is apostolic and that being so the language is 'we have seen and do testify'. '**We**' in verse 16, however, relates to the children of God and the language could not therefore be 'we have seen and do testify' but 'we have known and believed'. The perfect tense used in '**have known and believed**' indicates a past experience, the results of which remain with us to the present. The children of God have learned and accepted by faith the love that God has in us. That love was first to us as sinners but now it is that same love in us.

God's love to us in Christ has brought us into God's family and, abiding in the enjoyment of this love, we abide in the enjoyment of God finding a home in our heart and in our life.

4. 17   Herein is our love made perfect, that we may have boldness in the day of judgment: because as he is, so are we in this world.

In this section, from this verse to chapter 5 verse 3, it is the love of God perfected with us, v. 17. When the love of God is **made perfect** with us, we are assured of boldness in the future **day of judgement**, when the judgement of God in relation to his creatures will be exercised. We are thus viewed here as God's creatures, with responsibility to Him as creator.

John now introduces not the Holy Spirit of God but the Son of God, '**as he is, so are we in this world**'. Notice that it is not 'as he was' but 'as he is'. The day of judgement does not provoke fear in the believer because as God's Son is in heaven so are we in this world, beyond judgement.

4. 18   There is no fear in love; but perfect love casteth out fear: because fear hath torment. He that feareth is not made perfect in love.

There is no fear in connection with, and in the enjoyment of, the love which has been perfected with us, v. 17. **Perfect love** is love that has reached its goal, the love of God in all its fullness, and fear is expelled by it. Fear always has **torment**, but here it is torment particularly in relation to the day of judgement. Love perfected with us removes that fear and the torment connected with it.

In 1 John, it is primarily the love of God towards us which expresses itself in our compassion to the needy, in our obedience to His word and in many other respects. Though we do not have the expression 'the love of God' in chapter 4 verse 12, it does say that His love is perfected in us. The idea is that if we love one another, God's love toward us is perfected in us in that it has reached its desired effect in our lives. In this section, however, the love of God is perfected with us as we are assured of boldness in the day of judgement.

4. 19   We love him, because he first loved us.

The word 'him' is omitted; this love may embrace not only God but His whole purpose. We love, because He first loved us.

This expression '**first**' has already been expanded by John in verses 9, 10 and 14, where he speaks of the manner in which God first loved us. The teaching in verse 19 is that God moved in love toward us, else we had never loved Him or His family.

4. 20   If a man say, I love God, and hateth his brother, he is a liar: for he that loveth not his brother whom he hath seen, how can he love God whom he hath not seen?

In verse 19, we love, but, in verse 20, John speaks of a profession of love, when he says, 'If anyone say I love God'. If anyone says that he loves God and hates his brother, his profession is not just empty but is, in fact, a deliberate lie. The essential feature of a child of God is that he is a lover of God; this is characteristic of a Christian. In Romans chapter 8 verse 28, 'all things work together for good to them that love God'. In chapter 2 verses 9 and 11, the apostle says that he that 'hateth his brother is in darkness', whilst in chapter 3 verse 15, 'Whosoever hateth his brother is a murderer'. Now, John says that if a man says that he loves God and hates his brother he is a liar. It is impossible to love God and not to love your brother.

We have been told in verse 19 that a brother is loved by God, for He first loved us. The brother that has been loved by God is seen by us, though God who is the lover, has not been seen. John says, therefore, that '**he that loveth not his brother whom he hath seen**', who is the object of God's love, '**how can he love God whom he hath not seen?**'

4. 21   And this commandment have we from him, That he who loveth God love his brother also.

This matter of loving is a commandment from God. In verse 20, a brother loves because he is possessed of the new nature (he is my brother), but in verse 21 we love because of a commandment. This is something we are inclined to forget, that to love is a divine edict, a commandment. It might seem strange that we are commanded to love but this is necessary because of the flesh within us, which can make us envious and suspicious of each other.

When it is the matter of loving one's brother, it is not just an assumed relationship. We only speak of an assumed relationship when there are features which give evidence to the fact that he is not a regenerate person. A genuine brother could never be characterized by continual hatred.

Chapter 5

5. 1 **Whosoever believeth that Jesus is the Christ is born of God: and every one that loveth him that begat loveth him also that is begotten of him.**

The first three verses of chapter 5 are a continuation of the verses at the end of chapter 4. In chapter 4 verses 20 and 21, there is the matter of my loving my fellow Christian because of what he is to me; he is my brother. However, it is approached from a different standpoint in the first two verses of chapter 5, where I love my fellow Christian because of what he is to God. He has been begotten of God and is amongst the children of God.

In this verse it is important to observe that John is not telling us that it is a matter of believing in order to be **born of God**. He is not stating how it comes about that a person has been begotten of God but is simply saying that one of the evidences of having been born of God is believing that Jesus is the Christ. In the same way, in chapter 2 verse 29, doing righteousness is an evidence of having been born of God and, in chapter 4 verse 7, love is also an evidence of this.

In chapter 4 verses 2 and 15 the great matter is 'confessing that', but, in chapter 5, it is 'believing that', vv. 1 and 5, and believing 'in', vv. 10 and 13. In those verses the word 'on' translates the Greek preposition *eis*, which expresses movement towards the object; it is the activity of faith. 'Believing that' is believing facts, something that is merely passive. There is, therefore, a difference between 'believing that' and 'believing in'. Some say that there is no such difference, but the teaching here is that one cannot believe 'in' without believing 'that', although one can believe 'that' without believing 'in'.

In this verse, the one who has been begotten of God believes that **Jesus is the Christ**. The name Jesus speaks of his humanity, and Christ is the anointed one. This may have as its background the idea of the antichrist of which he has previously spoken.

The new birth is the divine standpoint, whilst believing is our standpoint. Dead people cannot believe. However, if you introduce a period of time, or the thought of sequence between the new birth and believing, you are treading on very dangerous ground. Some took the line of teaching that the priest, before he was sprinkled with blood, was washed with water. This also happened when the leper was cleansed. The washing with water speaks of the new birth and sprinkling with blood speaks of salvation. This is true, but the difficulty comes when we introduce a period of time between these two matters.

The difficulty has come in because in the transitional period in the book of the Acts there were those who had been born-again prior to the preaching of the Gospel of salvation in Christ. They enjoyed the new birth that belonged to an earthly people. Then, when they heard the message of salvation in Christ, they put their trust in Him. There was, at that time and in those circumstances, a difference, but we cannot read that difference into the present day because that transitional period is past.

5. 2   By this we know that we love the children of God, when we love God, and keep his commandments.

'**By this**' is 'herein'. When **we love God** and keep his commandments, we know that we love the children of God. If I love God who is the begetter, I love the children who have been begotten. This verse teaches that I know that I love the children of God when I love God; and there is added, significantly, '**and keep his commandments**'. If we do not keep His commandments, then our love for the children of God can be a pretended or spurious love. Our profession of love for a brother should obviously never condone or sanction what is not of God. This verse, then, is a warning against pretended love or love that might be purely sentimental its character.

5. 3   For this is the love of God, that we keep his commandments: and his commandments are not grievous.

Verse 2 teaches that if I do not love God's children I am disobedient to

God, but verse 3 teaches that if I do not love God I am also disobedient. Genuine love is always characterized by obedience. His commandments are not grievous, or heavy; they are not a burden.

Three important matters, 5. 4-21

1. Faith, vv. 4-13.
   Believing, vv. 5, 10, 13
2. Confidence, vv. 14-17.
   Asking, vv. 14, 15, 16
3. Assurance, vv.18-21.
   Knowing, vv. 18, 19, 20

Here we have three characteristics of the child of God. In verses 4 to 13, where the subject is faith, the keyword is 'believe'. Believing is simply the exercise of faith and the verb occurs in verses 5, 10 and 13. In verses 14 to 17, where the subject matter is confidence, the keyword is now 'ask'. The verb 'to ask' occurs three times, in verses 14, 15 and 16. In verses 18 to 21, where the subject matter is assurance, the keyword is 'know'. The word occurs in verses 18, 19 and 20 and has the idea of inward, conscious knowledge.

5. 4   **For whatsoever is born of God overcometh the world: and this is the victory that overcometh the world, even our faith.**

The thought of **the world** is introduced at this juncture because verse 3 has said that His commandments are not grievous; but if any of God's commandments are grievous and burdensome to us, it is because of succumbing to the influence of the world.

In verse 4, truth is presented in the abstract and, accordingly, the word used is '**whatsoever**', whereas in verse 5 it is truth in daily experience and so the word used is 'who'. The collective neuter, 'whatsoever', is the same idea that we have in John chapter 3 verse 6, where Jesus said, 'That which is born of the flesh is flesh; and that which is born of the Spirit is spirit'. In verse 1, the masculine is used, 'him that is begotten of God' but here it is '**whatsoever is born of God**'. It must be appreciated that it is not the person who achieves the victory but the power that is resident in the person by reason of his or her new birth. It is for this reason that the neuter gender is used here. It could equally be rendered 'all that is begotten of God', indicating that there are no exceptions in God's family in this matter. All in God's family are born of God by means of the new birth and all, therefore, have this power.

'**And this is the victory that overcometh the world**'. This is better rendered, 'overcame' the world. It is the aorist tense, pointing to a once for all victory, because it is truth stated in the abstract, a statement of doctrine.

The world was judged in the person of God's Son. In John chapter 16 verse 33, the Saviour said, 'be of good cheer; I have overcome the world'. He also had said, 'Now is the judgment of this world; now shall the prince of this world be cast out', John 12. 31. This is the world that wants our company but does not want our Saviour; that offers us prosperity but on its own terms, which are opposed to our faith; that offers us position but demands our allegiance.

It is **faith** that overcame, that gave the victory. It is only when we look beyond what is seen and temporal, which faith alone can do, and lay hold on that which is unseen and eternal, that there is this victory. This is, therefore, a tremendously important verse.

It is John's line of teaching both here and in Revelation that every Christian is an overcomer. Revelation chapter 21 verse 7 says, 'He that overcometh shall inherit all things; and I will be his God, and he shall be my son'. In the next verse, by way of contrast, he speaks of 'the fearful and unbelieving'. A person is either an overcomer or an unbeliever.

5. 5   Who is he that overcometh the world, but he that believeth that Jesus is the Son of God?

If in verse 4 we have truth in the abstract, in this verse we have it in daily experience, 'he that believeth'. It is not 'whatsoever', as in verse 4, but '**he that**'. 'He that' is masculine and '**overcometh**' is in the present tense. This verse is explanatory of verse 4. It is not now a person believing that Jesus is the Christ, as in verse 1, where His official glory is in view, but believing '**that Jesus is the Son of God**', which has in view His personal, divine, essential and eternal glory. It is the glory of such a person that makes everything in this world to recede.

The greatness of the person of the Son of God eclipses anything that the world might offer. Just as the sun extinguishes the shining of the stars, so the glory of the Son eclipses all that the world might offer. 'Whatsoever is born of God overcometh the world', that world system from which God and Christ have been excluded. There is no mention of the Father in this connection, although it is often said that the world is in opposition to the Father. Here, it is overcoming the world not by reason of the contrast with all that is involved with the Father but because of the greatness of the person of God's Son.

5. 6 **This is he that came by water and blood, even Jesus Christ; not by water only, but by water and blood. And it is the Spirit that beareth witness, because the Spirit is truth.**

'**This is he**' refers back to the Son of God in verse 5, where John has been directing our attention to His person; now, in verse 6, he directs our minds to His work.

The testimony, or **witness**, of God is concerning His Son coming to meet man's need. In the expression '**This is he that came by water and blood**'; 'by' is the Greek preposition *dia*, which means 'through', 'this is he that came through water and blood, Jesus Christ'. In the expression '**not by water only**' the Greek proposition changes to *en*; it should be rendered, 'not in the water only, but in the water and the blood'. This has the significance of, 'not in power of the water only but in power of the water and the blood'. I take it, therefore, that there are two matters; *dia* relates to the purpose of His coming and *en* relates to that purpose having been accomplished at Calvary. This may remind us of chapter 4 verses 2 and 3, where the idea of His coming in flesh is not limited to the incarnation but involves the fact and the purpose of it.

Some believe that these statements refer to our Lord's incarnation, the **water** and **blood** relating to His divine conception. However, in relation to His incarnation, the reference is never to water and blood but, rather, to blood and flesh. Hebrews chapter 2 verse 14 bears this out. 'Forasmuch then as the children are partakers of flesh and blood, he also himself likewise took part of the same; that through death he might destroy him that had the power of death, that is, the devil.' I suggest, therefore, that here it is not His incarnation that is in view but, rather, the purpose of His incarnation. He uses the past tense, this is He that 'came', which, together with '*dia* water and blood' signifies that John is giving a summing up of the purpose of His coming.

Others have suggested that 'water' refers to His baptism and 'blood' to His cross. They teach, generally, that coming 'through water' relates to His baptism, which marked the beginning of His public ministry, where there was a declaration of His deity as the Son of God. On that occasion the Father said, 'Thou art my beloved Son', Luke 3. 22. They also teach that the blood refers to His cross, which marked the termination of His ministry. However, this line of interpretation poses many problems. First of all, baptism is never symbolized by water. Peter says, in 1 Peter chapter 3 verses 20 and 21, 'God waited in the days of Noah, while the ark was a preparing, wherein few, that is, eight souls were saved by water. The like figure whereunto even baptism doth also now save us'. However, the water there refers to the deliverance from the judgement and not the water of baptism. Baptism is already a symbol; water would not be used as a symbol to explain what is, in fact, another symbol. Secondly, I would suggest that the beginning of His public ministry is connected not with His being the Son of God but with the fact that Jesus was the Christ. Luke chapter 4 verse 18 relates the beginning of His public ministry as the anointed one, but, in 1 John chapter 5 verses 5 and 6, Jesus Christ is the Son of God.

To those who relate the water here to His baptism as a testimony to His deity, the question might be asked, Why particularly His baptism? His deity was attested by far more than His baptism. At His incarnation the

Father said, 'Thou art my son, this day have I begotten thee'.[5] On the mount of transfiguration, Peter, James and John heard the Father say, 'This is my beloved Son', Matt. 17. 5; Mark 9. 7. Our Lord's deity was also attested by His raising of dead ones; He was 'declared to be the Son of God with power, according to the spirit of holiness, by the resurrection from the dead', Rom. 1. 4. It is unlikely that John would here just select His baptism as an attestation of His deity when it was also attested at His birth, His transfiguration, and in His raising people from the dead.

It almost seems to be irreverent to place alongside each other the water of Jordan and the blood that flowed from His pierced side. It may be for those who accept that interpretation that the witness of the Spirit confirms it. John says, '**and it is the spirit that beareth witness**' and on the occasion of His baptism the Spirit descended upon Him. John chapter 1 verse 33 says, 'Upon whom thou shalt see the Spirit descending, and remaining on him, the same is he which baptizeth with the Holy Ghost'. It must be observed, however, that in 1 John chapter 5 the Spirit bears witness not just to the water but also to the blood. This is important to note; we are certain of the witness of the Spirit at His baptism but there is no record of His witness on the occasion of the cross.

John speaks of the Spirit who '**beareth witness**', not who 'bore' witness. The fact that John is speaking of a present witness to the water and the blood, rather than of a past witness is, to my mind, conclusive in terms of the water and the blood speaking of the whole need of man being met by our Saviour's work at Calvary. The purpose of His coming was to meet man's need and this was accomplished. The Spirit does not bear witness either to His incarnation or His baptism meeting our need, something that would be dangerously near to accepting that the events of His life were atoning. The witness is to His death and His death alone meeting our need.

'**The Spirit is truth**'. When Jesus was here, He said, 'I am the truth', but John now says, 'the Spirit is the truth'. The Spirit operates on our hearts

---

[5] See: Ps. 2. 7; Acts 13. 33; Heb. 1. 5; 5. 5.

to make known the truth.

Man's need was twofold; he was dead and he was guilty, as chapter 4 verses 9 and 10 make clear. Verse 9 says, 'God sent his only begotten Son into the world, that we might live through him'. Water is a symbol of life and here speaks of life imparted, to effect moral cleansing. Verse 10 says, 'God . . . sent his Son to be the propitiation for our sins'. Blood is a symbol of life laid down, to effect judicial cleansing. Man is dead and needs the water of the new birth; he is guilty and needs the blood of expiation.

The water is the new birth, not eternal life. Eternal life is the result of the new birth. John uses water as a symbol of the word, and that is involved here as life is not dissociated from the word. In John chapter 3 verse 5, Jesus speaks to Nicodemus of the need to be 'born of water and of the Spirit'. New birth results from the Spirit by the word; 'water' is not the word by itself but the Spirit through the word.

John is the only writer of the four Gospels who mentions both the water and the blood in his Gospel. John speaks of the witness of men in verse 9; and John's private testimony to the water and blood is noted in John chapter 19 verse 35, where he says, 'And he that saw it bare record, and his record is true'. John, in a particular way, indicates that he saw it and bore testimony in order 'that ye might believe'. However, the present witness of God by the Spirit is greater. John witnessed it when it took place, but God, by the Spirit, bears witness now. The presence of blood and water when His side was pierced cannot be explained either medically or physically; it was divine and the explanation is here, water and blood symbolically meeting man's need.

The order in which water and blood is mentioned in this Epistle is different from John chapter 19. In John chapter 19, the order is blood and water, but here it is water and blood. In John's Gospel, things are viewed from the divine standpoint first and so the blood is mentioned before the water. In this Epistle, things are viewed first of all from the man-ward standpoint and so the order is reversed. The blood being mentioned first in the Gospel. indicates that God cannot move towards mankind until the blood was shed. As indicated earlier, water is connected with the new birth and blood is connected with expiation, and this is the order in which John presents truth in this Epistle, 4. 9, 10. In verse 9, the Son of God was sent in order that we might live, and this relates to the water. In verse 10, the Son of God was sent that He might be the propitiation, and this relates to the blood.

Water and blood is not a new thought. Immediately one entered into the court of the tabernacle, there was the brazen altar with its blood and the laver with its water. Thus, at the very commencement of one's experience in the tabernacle, one was confronted with blood and water. At the consecration of the priesthood, in Exodus chapter 29, the priests were first of all washed with water, then sprinkled with blood. At the cleansing of the leper, in Leviticus chapter 14, the leper washed himself first of all with water and then blood was sprinkled on his right ear, his right thumb and his right big toe. Water and blood also occur together in the New Testament. Hebrews chapter 10 verse 22 says, 'Let us draw near with a true heart in full assurance of faith, having our hearts sprinkled from an evil conscience, and our bodies washed with pure water'. Our hearts are sprinkled from an evil conscience, which is the action of blood; our bodies are washed with pure water. 1 Corinthians chapter 6 verse 11 says, 'And such were some of you: but ye are washed, but ye are sanctified, but ye are justified in the name of the Lord Jesus, and by the Spirit of our God'. 'Ye are washed' is the action of water; 'ye are justified and sanctified' is the action of blood.

The soldier in John chapter 19 did not shed His blood. No shedding of blood by man could effect remission. Christ shed His own blood internally on the tree, so that when the soldier pierced His side He was already dead. He had already voluntarily shed His own blood. The soldier piercing His side was intended to give an external witness to something that had already happened. When Hebrews chapter 9 verse 22 says, 'without shedding of blood is no remission', it does not refer to the act of the soldier but to Christ's own act in shedding His blood. Earlier in John chapter 19, in verse 28, it says that Jesus knew 'that all things were now accomplished', and then cried, 'It is finished'. He did not need to cry this, in that He knew it already, but did so as an external witness. Some suggest that the presence of water indicates that He died of a broken heart, but blood and water cannot be explained medically or physically; rather, it was divine. Man being guilty needed the blood and being dead he needed the water.

The flowing of blood and water from His side was an evidence that He was a real man but also provided a testimony as to His deity. It has been said that if you pierce the side of a dead man one thousand times blood will never flow out. The first thing to congeal upon death is blood; He was more than mere man.

The shedding of the blood in John chapter 19 had two things in view. Verses 34 and 35 say, 'But one of the soldiers with a spear pierced his side, and forthwith came there out blood and water. And he that saw it bare record, and his record is true; and he knoweth that he saith true, that ye might believe'. The side was pierced, and forthwith came there out blood and water, as a witness that we might believe now and for the future awakening of the nation of Israel, when they shall look upon Him whom they pierced.

5. 7 For there are three that bear record in heaven, the Father, the Word, and the Holy Ghost: and these three are one.

There is a widely held view that the words 'in heaven, the Father, the Word, and the Holy Ghost: and these three are one. And there are three that bear witness in earth' should be omitted. One has said that such a witness is not required in heaven. The elect and the holy angels do not need a witness as to that which will meet their need; and the spirits of the saints who are now in heaven do not require such a witness. Of course, when you understand the witness as witnessing to man's need being fully met then you can understand there is no need for witness in heaven. The fact that Christ is there is all the witness that is necessary to man's need having been met.

5.8 **And there are three that bear witness in earth, the Spirit, and the water, and the blood: and these three agree in one.**

Now here there is a remarkable thing; the order is reversed. In verse 6, there is the water, the blood and the Spirit, but here the order of the three that bear witness is '**the Spirit, and the water, and the blood**'. This is tremendously important. In verse 6 is the historical order; there is Calvary first, the water and the blood, and then the Spirit. Calvary, historically, preceded the Spirit being sent down to bear witness. In verse 8, however, it is not to do with the historical order but the dealings of God with the souls of men. The Spirit comes first because it is to do with divine dealings in the soul. He first deals with the soul of man and then there is the application of that which meets man's need, the water and the blood.

The Spirit is, of course, the only personal witness. The water and the blood are figurative witnesses, though they are here personified. The witnesses are not bearing witness to themselves but to the fact that here alone can man's need be met.

The literal rendering of '**these three agree in one**' is, 'these three are into one'. The thought is that these three have one object, which is to bear witness to the truth. To that they give a united testimony.

5.9 **If we receive the witness of men, the witness of God is greater: for this is the witness of God which he hath testified of his Son.**

In verses 9 and 10, there are another three witnesses, 'the witness of men', 'the witness of God' and, in verse 10, 'the witness in himself'.

In '**if we receive the witness of men**', John is not questioning the witness of men; it is accepted that the witness of men concerning these matters has been received. However, **the witness of God is greater**. It is greater in that God fully knows the value of Christ and His work. Men can speak about it, but we do not rest on what men say; we rest on God's estimate, and thus the witness of God, which is concerning His Son, is greater.

5. 10 **He that believeth on the Son of God hath the witness in himself: he that believeth not God hath made him a liar; because he believeth not the record that God gave of his Son.**

This is now the third witness, '**He that believeth on the Son of God hath the witness in himself**'. This is the first occurrence of believing on the Son of God, presented here as an object of faith. The witness is not just the Son and not just eternal life but the Son and eternal life, because of the wording of verse 12, 'He that hath the Son hath life'. The proof of receiving Christ is that we rest upon Him, which we cannot do without having received Him. We do not receive the Lord as Saviour and feel that if that fails something else might do; we receive the person as our only hope of salvation.

The Son indwells the believer. In John chapter 14 verse 20, the Lord Jesus said, 'At that day ye shall know that I am in my Father, and ye in me, and I in you'. Also, in verse 23 He said, 'If a man love me, he will keep my words: and my Father will love him, and we will come unto him, and make our abode with him'.

'**He that believeth not God hath made him a liar**'. It says, he that believeth 'on' the Son of God but he that believeth 'not God'. To believe on the Son is to believe God's testimony; not to believe God is not to believe in His Son. In '**because he believeth not the record that God gave of his Son**' a past tense is employed; 'hath believed not' involves permanent results. To reject God's testimony of His Son is a serious matter, for it makes God a liar. In chapter 1 verse 10, it is to do with God lying about me but here with God telling lies about His Son.

5. 11 **And this is the record, that God hath given to us eternal life, and this life is in his Son.**

'**The record**' or 'the witness' is '**that God hath given to us eternal life**'. Paul also says, in Romans chapter 6 verse 23, that eternal life is 'the gift of God'. John says, '**this life is in his Son**'; Paul says that it is 'in Jesus Christ our Lord'.

5. 12 **He that hath the Son hath life; and he that hath not the Son of God hath not life.**

'**He that hath the Son hath life**', the life that John has been talking about. '**And he that hath not the Son of God hath not life**'. The verse is just explanatory of verse 11. To have the Son is to have life; and it is impossible to have the one without the other.

5. 13 **These things have I written unto you that believe on the name of the Son of God; that ye may know that ye have eternal life, and that ye may believe on the name of the Son of God.**

The verse might be rendered, 'These the things I wrote to you, that ye may know that ye that believe on the name of the Son of God have eternal life'. He is not writing in order that they might believe but that they might know that having believed they have eternal life.

The name stands for all that Christ is and all that He has done. To believe on His name is to repose by faith on the truth of His person and the work that He accomplished at the place called Calvary.

5. 14 **And this is the confidence that we have in him, that, if we ask any thing according to his will, he heareth us:**

'**In him**' is 'toward him' and '**confidence**' is 'boldness'. 'This is the boldness we have toward him'. The word boldness has occurred previously in this Epistle. John expresses his confidence in relation to the future, 2. 28; 4. 17, and his confidence in relation to the present, 3. 21; 5. 14.

To **ask** is in the sense of supplicating and this **confidence** is the boldness that accepts that if we ask according to His will God hears us. Asking according to His will involves our own will being completely excluded; we seek only the will of God. The prayer here is individual and what is stated is true of all in God's family. In verse 16, where there is a specific request in view, it changes to 'he' but in this verse it is 'we', as what is general is in view.

We must remember that it is God's word alone that acquaints us with what is the will of God. There is no purpose, reason or sense in asking something that the word of God says would be wrong for me. For instance, if a young man was interested in an unconverted young lady there is no need to ask guidance for that because he ought to know from God's word that it is not according to God's will.

In relation to prayer there is the prayer of faith and the prayer of submission. The prayer of faith assures us that we are asking according to His will. An example of this is in James chapter 5, where the prayer of faith will save the sick. Where the word of God does not speak directly about the matter concerning which we are praying, our prayer is to be not the prayer of faith but the prayer of submission, which says, 'if it be according to Thy will'. Here it is the will of God as it affects our daily lives.

David was a man after God's own heart in that God desired a place to dwell in and David desired the same thing. Paul's prayer in 2 Corinthians chapter 12, regarding the thorn in the flesh, was a prayer of submission. When he received the answer that the thorn would not be removed but that sufficient grace would be supplied, he submitted to the will of God. There are certain things, then, about which we may pray the prayer of faith knowing full well that they are according to the scriptures and that it is the will of God. However, matters like Paul's thorn in the flesh would be a prayer of submission to the will of God, waiting for God to declare what is in fact His will. The great thing is to come humbly before God. We must also remember that the hearing of the petition is not the same as it being granted. When Paul prayed three times that the thorn in the flesh might be removed, God heard him. However, He did not grant him the removing of the thorn but all the grace that was necessary in the circumstances.

'Praying in the Holy Ghost', Jude 20, comes under the category of things mentioned in Romans chapter 8 for which the Spirit maketh intercession for us. This is one instance in which the Spirit undertakes for us. Of course, you could not divorce the activity of the Spirit in one's life from a knowledge of the will of God.

The Lord Jesus said, 'I knew that thou hearest me always', John 11. 42. Here was one who was never out of touch; the Father always heard Him. In connection with this, there is a very important statement in Hebrews chapter 5 verse 7, which states that He 'was heard in that he feared' or He 'was heard on account of his piety'.

Prayer is not necessarily expressed in words. In fact, one can be praying without being actually conscious of it. Someone has said, the language of prayer can be deeper than consciousness.

5. 15 **And if we know that he hear us, whatsoever we ask, we know that we have the petitions that we desired of him.**

'**If**' can be rendered since. '**Desired**' is the same word as 'asked' in verse 14; '**know**' is inward consciousness, so there can be no doubt. If we have inward consciousness that He hears us, we have inward consciousness that we have the petitions that we desired. It does not say that 'we shall have' the petitions but that 'we have' them; we know that they have already been granted. It might not be obvious as yet but we have the inward assurance that they have already been granted. This inward consciousness can only come from God and, seeing as it is not in the future tense, it would indicate that it comes at the time of the petition. Inward consciousness of being in the will of God can be the enjoyed portion of any in the family of God.

5. 16 **If any man see his brother sin a sin which is not unto death, he shall ask, and he shall give him life for them that sin not unto death. There is a sin unto death: I do not say that he shall pray for it.**

There are many ideas on this verse and it is not without its problems.

First of all, note that it is a hypothetical case. He says, '**If** any man see his brother'. Notice also the word '**see**'; observation is involved. Further, it is a course pursued because '**sin a sin**' is 'sinning a sin'.

'**Not unto death**' is the same expression as used in John chapter 11 verse 4 in respect of the sickness of Lazarus, a sickness not necessarily issuing in death. So, the sense is, 'If any man observe his brother sinning a sin which does not necessarily issue in death'. In those early days discipline that resulted in death was characteristic of God's dealings with men in the church. 1 Corinthians chapter 11 verse 30 says, 'For this cause many are weak and sickly among you, and many sleep'. Again, in James chapter 5, there is a sickness that could result in death but the man was delivered from it.

'**He shall ask**' is connected to the previous verses of asking according to God's will and having the petitions that we desire. 'He shall ask', therefore, involves asking according to God's will. 'Ask' is the same word we have been considering in verses 14 and 15, in the sense of entreaty and supplication. The result of the asking by the brother who sees will effect repentance in the heart of the brother who has sinned a sin not unto death.

Thus, if we see a brother sinning, we do not gossip about the matter to the brother's discredit, as the flesh in us might want to do, but we take that matter to God in prayer, having in our hearts the brother's recovery. What would issue from that is the possibility of counselling the sinning brother, but the first step is asking.

'**And he shall give him life**'. The word employed is not one that John employs regarding physical life. This expression involves more than physical life because it is the restoration of the enjoyment of his spiritual life. This is much higher than simply being saved from physical death. I tend to think it is the idea that Paul mentions in 1 Thessalonians chapter 3 verse 8, where he says, 'For now we live, if ye stand fast in the Lord'. There are conditions that can hinder our enjoyment of spiritual life.

'**There is a sin unto death**'. Physical death in this instance seems to be inevitable, unavoidable. Some, because of this, have suggested that the sin here is the sin of murder as this makes death inevitable, if punishment is carried out according to God, Gen. 9. 6. Others have suggested that the sin unto death might have the significance that the effects of a particular sin remain until death, such as in the case of divorce and remarriage, the sin of adultery perhaps involving illegitimate offspring.

I tend to think, however, that the thought is that the sin itself, rather than its effects, is irreversible. Here is a particular sin for which there is no forgiveness, such as the sin of apostasy. To deny Jesus Christ come in the flesh and, v. 10, to make God a liar is the sin of this particular Epistle; it is irreversible and issues in death. It is the same as in Hebrews chapter 10 verses 26 and 27. An apostate is a man in spiritual death, which leads to eternal death.

I rather think that this does not refer to a case such as that of Ananias and Sapphira, where there are unique circumstances. God was acting in those early days, before the scriptures were completed as we have them now, to preserve the church in its purity. In 1 Corinthians chapter 11, as previously noted, God retains that prerogative to act in government towards His people.

'**I do not say**'. John is not giving a command to pray but says, 'I do not say he shall pray'. '**Pray**', a different word from 'ask', implies familiarity. It can also be rendered, 'ask for information' and can even imply equality. Thus, the asking in connection with the sin not unto death is petitioning or supplicating but in respect of sin unto death it is questioning, asking for information. Notice, also, that it does not say and he shall 'pray for him' but that he shall '**pray for it**', information in connection with a particular sin.

The contrast, then, between the beginning and the end of the verse is that we should pray for the brother at the beginning but there is no need to pray concerning the person at the end, who is an apostate. The word '**brother**' is used of an assumed relationship. If the reference is to one possessed of the spirit of Antichrist he has taken up an assumed position.

In 2 Timothy, there is a difference between Alexander the Coppersmith on the one hand and Hymenaeus and Alexander on the other. In respect of the latter two it was a case of blasphemy; excommunication was involved in order that they might learn, in the sphere outside of divine influence, not to blaspheme. That was an apostolic act. In 2 Timothy chapter 4 verse 14, Paul says, 'Alexander the coppersmith did me much evil; the Lord will reward him according to his works'. Paul is not praying that the Lord will deal with him but rather that Alexander had done something against him and he would leave him to the Lord to deal with. What Paul says is not imprecatory in character.

5. 17 All unrighteousness is sin: and there is a sin not unto death.

The word is 'every' **unrighteousness is sin**. Let us not lose the weight of this on our hearts and souls. Every act of mine that is not consistent with the mind and will of God is sin. This is, of course, a warning against lack of diligence in our Christian life day by day.

It is also helpful to consider what John has to say about sin elsewhere in this Epistle. He tells us what sin is in chapter 3 verse 4, where he says that 'sin is the transgression of the law'. The rendering of the verse is, 'Whosoever doeth sin doeth also lawlessness: and sin is lawlessness'. The expression 'the transgression of the law' would almost make us think that John is here speaking about transgressing the law of Moses, but the verse is to do with both the Jew under the law and the Gentile not under the law. The word is really 'lawlessness'. It is neither a question of having the law and disregarding it nor one of never having been under the law. Sin is lawlessness, which is simply self-will, self-pleasing and acting in independence of God. In chapter 3 verse 5, John says, 'he was manifested to take away our sins; and in him is no sin'. John is not there pointing out how sin would be taken away but that sin is so hateful to God that God says it must be taken away, even at the expense of one in whom is no sin at all. John makes it very clear throughout his Epistle that our attitude to sin determines where we stand in relation to God, whether we know Him or do not know Him.

5. 18 We know that whosoever is born of God sinneth not; but he that is begotten of God keepeth himself, and that wicked one toucheth him not.

In verse 18 we are told that the child of God is one who has been born of God; in verse 19 we are told that the child of God is of God; and in verses 20 and 21 we are told that the child of God is in God. Here then are three lovely expressions: born of God, v. 18; of God, v. 19; and in God, vv. 20, 21.

In verse 18, the subject matter is the child of God and the evil one. In verse 19, the subject matter is the world and the evil one. Then, verses 20 and 21, the subject matter is the true God and idols.

'**We know**' means that we have this inward knowledge that everyone who has been born of God '**sinneth not**'. This is strange after what John has said in verse 16 about seeing a brother sinning. We have seen before that it is necessary in studying the Epistle by John to observe the tenses. Here, it is the present continuous tense, meaning 'sinneth not habitually'. The difference between verses 16 and 18 is that in verse 16 it is the exception but in verse 18 it is the habit.

'**But he that is begotten of God keepeth himself.**' The question to decide here is whether the word '**himself**' should be 'himself' or 'him'. In the Greek language, there is only one letter that distinguishes the two words. The expression '**he that is begotten of God**' is most unusual, as the apostle uses the aorist tense. With regard to the children of God, he always uses the perfect tense, 'he that hath been begotten of God', as at the beginning of the verse. The perfect tense refers to something that took place in the past and continues in the present, and this is true of every child of God. The aorist tense, however, is simply a statement of fact without necessarily referring to time. Accordingly, 'the begotten of God' does not refer to the child of God but to Christ Himself.

The begotten of God, Christ, **keepeth** not 'himself' but 'him', the believer. Therefore, the Apostle John is speaking about the keeping power of the Son of God, the outcome being that the evil one toucheth him not. The power is not in us to keep ourselves; the keeping power is of God and of His Son. The word for 'keep' means to watch over, to keep an eye on, to observe attentively. It is the same word as in John chapter 17 verse 12, when the Lord said, 'those that thou gavest me I have kept'. This is what Christ does constantly; there is never a moment when His eye is not on us. For this reason, the devil cannot touch us.

The idea in the word '**toucheth**' is not 'touch at all' but 'touch vitally'. The believer is kept, not from the attack but from being affected vitally by the evil one. As Peter says, 'And who is he that will harm you, if ye be followers of that which is good?' 1 Peter 3. 13. Christians are not beyond being harmed but they are beyond being vitally harmed.

5. 19   And we know that we are of God, and the whole world lieth in wickedness.

The thought is that 'the whole world lieth in the evil one'. The verse contrasts the conscious knowledge and assurance of the child of God with the ignorance and unconscious complacency of the world.

We know that we are of God means that we have this conscious knowledge that we are of God. '**Of God**' refers to the source, that we are begotten of God. We also know that the whole world lieth in the evil one. Thus, there is the child of God and the whole world, and there is no in-between. '**Lieth**' has the idea of lying unconcernedly in the evil one. In verse 20, we are in Him that is true; but the whole world lieth unconcernedly and complacently in the evil one.

5. 20   And we know that the Son of God is come, and hath given us an understanding, that we may know him that is true, and we are in him that is true, even in his Son Jesus Christ. This is the true God, and eternal life.

'**We know**' is, again, conscious knowledge. **We know that the Son of God came.** It is a perfect tense; this refers to the incarnation of Christ being inwardly known and consciously appreciated. He '**hath given us an understanding**', which embraces such things as intellectual powers and the faculty of moral reflection, that we may know the true one. The true one is God, who is '**the only true God**'. 'That we may know' is expressed in the present tense; we have the possession of this knowledge and there is the progression as we continually know the true one. We also '**are in him that is true**' and so we know the Father and we are in Him. 'We know Him' is recognition; 'we are in Him' is security.

'**Even**' is omitted and there is a new statement, '**in his son Jesus Christ**'. In the previous statement, it is the true one and now, His Son. Not 'the' Son but 'his' Son, the Son of the true one. We are, then, not only in the Father but we are in His Son, of whom John says, '**This is the true God, and eternal life**'. The true God speaks of Christ's deity; eternal life is rather His humanity, in the sense that eternal life is secured in Him as a risen man.

The true God is in contrast to both false gods and inferior gods. In the Old Testament the judges are called gods, as are angels; these are inferior gods. He is also the true God in contrast to false gods, the gods of man's making.

All the heresies which were in the early days of the church are repeated in these last days. To a large extent, many of these were virtually non-existent for many centuries but they have been revived in our day. I often times feel that ministry on God Himself, the deity of Christ and the Holy Spirit does not appeal to many. Many of the saints would rather have a pep talk, some practical ministry, and yet there needs to be a restatement of these fundamental truths.

5. 21   Little children, keep yourselves from idols. Amen.

The word '**keep**' is different from the word used earlier on. Here the word is 'guard' or 'defend' yourselves from idols. '**Idols**' simply refers to every object outside of Christ that displaces Him in our affections and loyalty and to which we might cleave. Satan makes that into an idol. We are to guard ourselves from these, which means we are not to tamper with them.